TALES
FROM THE
PRINCIPAL'S OFFICE
Case Studies in School Administration

TALES FROM THE PRINCIPAL'S OFFICE

Case Studies in School Administration

Marilyn Hogg
Marilyn Merler

Pacific Educational Press • Vancouver, British Columbia

Published by Pacific Educational Press
Faculty of Education, University of British Columbia
6365 Biological Sciences Road, Vancouver, BC, Canada V6T 1Z4
Telephone: 604-822-5385; Facsimile: 604-822-6603
Email: pep@interchange.ubc.ca

Library and Archives Canada Cataloguing in Publication

Hogg, Marilyn, 1954–
   Tales from the principal's office: case studies in school administration /
Marilyn Hogg, Marilyn Merler

ISBN 978-1-895766-86-8

   1. School management and organization--Canada--Case studies.
   2. Elementary school administration—Canada—Case Studies.
   I. Merler, Marilyn, 1957– II. Title.

LB2831.9.H63 2007   371.200971   C2007-901049-0

Copyediting by Laraine Coates
Cover design by Warren Clark

Printed and bound in Canada

Cover image: Laraine Coates

Contents

Contents

Contents

Introduction

——·—

As brand new school principals with newly acquired master's degrees in administration, we felt that we were prepared to meet the challenges of our jobs. After all, we thought to ourselves, anyone who had studied that much administrative theory should be ready to solve any problem. But we found that on the job we also needed a practical approach that would help us cope with and solve the numerous issues that arose everyday.

We realized that we needed to take time out to think about our decisions and to talk to other administrators about the issues that we faced. We started a study group with two other principals who were also new to the job. Each member of the group wrote about a problem that had been challenging in the past month and shared it with the other members for their input. Some problems were ongoing, and some problems had already been dealt with, but the discussions were nevertheless always valuable. After about six months of meeting, we considered writing a book of case studies that would be based on the problems encountered by school administrators in Canada. Two of us had the commitment and determination to see the book project through to the end. Thus, it became a reality.

The job of the administrator at any school is complex and multi-faceted. The school principal must be able to balance the wants, needs, and desires of staff, students, parents, and community members while ensuring a balanced budget and the delivery of a quality and equitable education program for all students. He or she must also make sure that various union contracts are upheld, that school board policies and Ministry of Education directives are followed, and that all media inquiries are answered expediently. The myriad of daily decisions that a school administrator must make requires both a strong knowledge base and effective decision-making skills. This book offers new principals, aspiring principals, and practising principals a way to explore issues and to engage in problem solving so that they can build this knowledge base and develop their decision-making skills.

This book is thus not meant to be a theoretical text but rather an opportunity to consider some of the real-life challenges that an administrator might face. It is written to give you time to think about the theoretical knowledge that you have and explore how it can be applied to solve practical problems that could occur in a school.

This book is best used as a focal point for group discussion since one of the challenges for many new principals is the isolation of the job. We have tried to present case studies that reflect some of the recurring issues principals face: student safety, bullying, poverty, parental involvement, increasing complexity of the family, cultural fairness, decreasing budgets and increasing expectations, and union relations. Each problem is described, but in many cases, a possible resolution or outcome is not included with the case. This provides an opportunity to discuss the situation and to problem-solve by asking: "What would I do in this situation?" We have also developed questions for each case study to help stimulate discussion. For some problems one encounters as a principal, there is no right or wrong answer, and there is often more than one solution. In the appendix at the back of the book, the reader is provided with one possible outcome for the situations that do not contain the resolution as part of the text. There is also a series of mini-cases following the larger case studies intended to generate further discussion.

As you read the book and discuss the case studies, it is important to keep in mind that there are references, in addition to educational theory, that can be used to help inform your decision-making process. These resources include your provincial school act, provincial human rights act, local school district policy, local collective agreements, and provincial professional codes of ethics for teachers and principals, support staff, and district office personnel.

The book is arranged so that it follows the school year—the case studies reflect the activities that typically happen starting in September and ending in June. The book centres on the problems encountered by a fictional principal named Janice Wright and her staff at the fictitious Harmony Elementary School. The school is located on a busy street close to the downtown area in a small city. Three hundred and fifty students attend the dual track school, and half of the students are in the French Immersion program. As you read about the problems that Principal Wright and Vice-Principal Simard encounter, keep these three questions in mind:

- What is the real issue?
- Whose needs must be met?
- Where could I go to get the information I need to make a decision?

If principals develop the habit of looking at situations through a frame of questions needing answers, it will make their decision-making process easier. When making decisions, it is important to remember that schools are primarily a place of learning for students, not a place of employment for adults. Students and their needs must come first.

When dealing with issues at school, we sometimes feel the pressure to make a decision right away. In most cases, remember that it is fine to take the time you need to think things over, consult the appropriate documents, or talk it over with a colleague. Give yourself permission to say, "Let me get back to you on that" or "I need some time to think about that."

Introduction

We hope that you will use this book in the spirit in which it was intended—not to provide precise answers, but to give you a focal point for discussion with other aspiring and practising school-based administrators. We want this book to encourage you to take:

- time to make a decision;
- time to talk through the issues with colleagues;
- time to reflect; and
- time to get the information you need before making a decision.

This book is our gift of time to you. We hope that you enjoy it!

Marilyn & Marilyn

The CASE STUDIES

1

I AM NOT RACIST!

―――・+・―――

It was just one week before the start of school, and Janice Wright, the principal of Harmony Elementary, was looking forward to the challenges of a new school year. Since the school secretary was on her lunch break, Janice picked up the phone and cheerfully answered, "Harmony Elementary School, Janice Wright speaking, how may I help you?" She listened in disbelief as Mr. Turner, one of her grade 6 teachers, told her that he had just been diagnosed with Parkinson's disease and would not be able start the school year. He said that he was hopeful that he would be able to return to the school by January or February, but until then he would need to be replaced. Janice felt overwhelmed as she contemplated both what this diagnosis meant for her staff member as well as what it would mean to the students who were looking forward to being in Mr. Turner's class. He was one of the most liked teachers at Harmony Elementary.

Janice phoned the head of human resources, told him what was happening with Mr. Turner, and explained that she would need a "really good replacement." He replied that he would see what he could do but that the job would go to the qualified person with the most seniority. Janice was hopeful that she would get a suitable replacement teacher and that the year would be a good one for the students in grade 6 at Harmony.

Since the job had to be posted for one week, the replacement teacher was not hired until the Friday before the last long weekend of summer. Janice did not meet the new teacher, Ms. Gillespie, until the morning of the first day of school, but she did notice that Ms. Gillespie had been in to the school on the weekend to prepare for the upcoming school year and her room was ready to go. When Janice first noticed her in the staffroom, she was struck by how unhappy Ms. Gillespie looked. As she went up to introduce herself, Ms. Gillespie looked her in the eye and said hello but did not smile. Janice said that she was happy to welcome her to Harmony Elementary School and encouraged Ms. Gillespie to let her know if there was anything that she needed. Ms. Gillespie said that things were fine and that she was happy to be at the school, and then she walked away. Janice wondered if she should have asked her if anything was wrong but decided to leave her alone for the time being. On that first day, the students arrived at 10:00 a.m. and were dismissed at 12:30 p.m. While the students were there, Janice stood outside Ms. Gillespie's room to observe. Janice noticed that when she was talking to the students she was positive, but that she did not often smile. Janice was starting to wonder if her newest teacher really wanted to be there.

The first week went by and Janice heard only one complaint about Ms. Gillespie. It came from the Aboriginal student support worker, Joe Rae, who was in the class half-time to assist three Aboriginal students. He reported that Ms. Gillespie did not seem to want to help the Aboriginal students and did not seem comfortable having him in her class. Janice said that she would give Ms. Gillespie some time to settle in and then she would be in to check on the class.

One week later after school, a very angry Joe Rae rushed into Janice's office. He exclaimed, "That teacher is a racist and she has to go!" Janice asked him to describe what had happened. He said that he had been helping the three students that he usually worked with on their math. Two of the boys had been fooling around and not listening to him and did not get their work done. Ms. Gillespie told him that he was too nice and he was providing too much help to the students and that was why they were not listening to him. She had then instructed the boys to take the math home as homework. He had followed the boys out into the hallway to make sure that they each took their homework with them. When he re-entered the classroom, Ms. Gillespie said, "You know they won't grow up to be lazy Indians if we make them behave and help them to develop a work ethic." He stopped, stared at her, and said, "What right do you have to talk to me about those students that way?" She replied, "I have Indian heritage and I was raised in poverty and I know that hard work will make those boys successful. We have to make them accountable and not put up with their nonsense."

At that point, Joe was too angry to say anything so he left and came straight to Janice. Janice could not believe that a teacher on her staff would ever say something like that to anyone, but, then again, she did not really know Ms. Gillespie. She decided that it was time she got to know her.

Discussion Questions

* Is the teacher guilty of racism?
* What factors should the principal consider when handling this situation?
* What do you think should happen to the teacher?

See appendix, page 129

2

SPLIT DECISIONS

Janice Wright knew that this was going to happen. Here they were, on the first day of school, having to reorganize the classes. At the end of June in the previous school year, she and her teachers had allowed for very little movement in the grade 1 to 3 classes in an effort to avoid combined classes. Now they were two students over the limit in the grade 3 class, but they had to adhere to class size regulations. They would have to reorganize. Janice and the grade 1 to 3 teachers met after school. Using the updated numbers, they worked together to redistribute the students and create new divisions. They all agreed that creating a grade 2–3 combined class from one of the grade 2 classes was the most viable option. The other classes would remain single grade classes.

Next, they had to determine who would teach the combined class, so Janice asked for volunteers. No one volunteered.

Harmony Elementary was a large school and historically had been able to avoid combined classes. On the rare occasion when there had been a combined class, the last person not to have had a combined class would teach it. It would be "their turn." Janice wasn't particularly comfortable with this practice, which her predecessor had established. She hoped that an acceptable volunteer would come forward. Janice remarked that perhaps they needed some time to think about it. She talked with the teachers about the kind of support they could expect, and they discussed the pros and cons of combined classes. Janice said that they would keep the original divisions in place for the following day and meet again after school. If no one volunteered, she would choose someone.

The teachers reminded her whose turn it was. In Janice's opinion, this teacher, Mrs. Murphy, was a marginal teacher who had some organizational and rapport problems. She was also experiencing some family problems with her teenaged son. Janice was not sure that she would be able to do a very good job of handling the combined class. The students were her main concern. If no one volunteered, she would choose the best person for the job. That evening, she dug up several articles extolling the virtues of combined classes. She made copies and put them into all of the teachers' mailboxes.

The following afternoon, the grade 1 to 3 teachers met again. Janice asked if they had had a chance to read the information she had given them about combined classes. They said that they had. She then asked if anyone would volunteer to teach the combined class. After a long and suspenseful silence, no one stepped forward and so Janice informed them whom she had chosen. She explained that it was her decision and it did not have to be based on whose "turn" it was. She had made her decision based on what would be best for the students. She had chosen Mr. Evans, an experienced grade 3 teacher who had been at the school for many years. He had a good reputation within the parent community as a solid teacher, and Janice knew that he would do a good job.

"It's not my turn!" exclaimed Mr. Evans. "I don't want that class! I'm going to see the president of the teachers' union!" He stood up and stomped out of the meeting. The rest of the staff sat with their mouths open. This was a side of Mr. Evans they had never seen. The meeting was quickly adjourned, and the teachers hurried out of the room.

Discussion Questions

* How should teaching assignments be determined? Should school history play a part?

- What rights do teachers have in determining their assignments?
- What is the principal's role in assigning teaching duties?

See appendix, page 129

3

WHO IS RESPONSIBLE HERE?

It was the beginning of the school year. Not only did Janice Wright have to contend with the usual September headaches, but she was also in the middle of a construction site. Walls were being torn down and replaced, and carpenters, painters, plumbers, and electricians were everywhere. Staff morale was low, and parents were concerned about student safety. Janice didn't even have an office to go to, to try to sort things out.

September and October came and went. Soon it was November, and the school was still nowhere near completion. Janice found that a good deal of her administration time was spent dealing with construction issues. Each morning she spent at least a half-hour doing a safety tour of the school to make sure that students would not be harmed by any of the equipment or construction activities that were to take place that day. She and the vice-principal, Doug Simard, had found several unsafe practices while on these tours—for example, an electric saw left unattended, wires hanging out of the ceiling, extension cords and ladders across main hallways, and fire doors left propped open. The administrators had to be vigilant throughout the course of the day; for example, they once had to remind the project foreman that recess was not an acceptable time for a crane to deliver drywall. The workers were co-operative and generally careful. However, it was difficult to predict what an elementary student might do.

One day, the workers were moving a bank of eight large open wooden lockers with coat hooks from one part of the school to another. It was close to lunch, and the classroom where the lockers were supposed to go was not yet ready for them. So, the workers placed the lockers in the middle of the hallway. They reasoned that the lockers were fairly stable and they wouldn't be there long. The lunch bell rang, and the students left their classrooms to go to get their lunches from their lockers. The grade 1 class was curious about the bank of new lockers sitting in the middle of the hall but the lunch supervisor told the students to stay away.

Josh, an active grade 1 boy, was intrigued. When the supervisor left to continued on her rounds, he couldn't resist swinging from one hook to the other. He was having a grand time, until the bank of lockers came crashing down, pinning Josh on the floor, and hitting his classmate's shoulder. Josh's screams quickly brought the supervisor to his rescue, and, with the help of two teachers, she freed Josh from under the lockers. The first-aid attendant and the principal were summoned. Josh had been hit on the back of the head and on his back by the lockers. There was a lot of blood, and Josh was extremely upset. Fortunately, he was not seriously injured. His classmate Jessica's shoulder had received quite a gash, but she was also going to be all right. She just wanted her parents.

Janice was shaking. She felt sick. She knew that the injuries could have been a lot worse. They were very lucky. She had been so careful about safety on the construction site, and she felt she had done everything she could to prevent such an accident from happening. Although she knew the accident was not her fault, she felt she had let her students down. She had the task of phoning their parents to explain to them what had happened. The parents came to pick up their children to take them to their family doctors. Janice apologized, and the parents and students left, thankful that the injuries were not more serious.

By this time, the lunch hour was over and the foreman was back from lunch. Janice told him what had happened. He told her that he already knew because some of his workers had informed him of the accident. He admitted that leaving the lockers in the middle of the hall was a bad idea on the part of his workers. He also explained that they were auxiliary workers and were not used to working in a school setting. They had wrongly assumed that they could leave the lockers there and the lockers would remain undisturbed while they went for lunch. The foreman apologized and said that he would speak to the workers. He assured Janice that this would not happen again. Janice knew that they would not leave a bank of lockers in the middle of the hallway again, but what might they do next?

After Josh recovered, his parents wrote a letter to the superintendent about the safety issues at Harmony Elementary. Janice was asked to attend a meeting between Josh's parents, the superintendent, and the maintenance supervisor at the school board office. Everyone apologized to Josh's parents and assured them that this kind of oversight would not happen again.

The following week, a sheet of plywood was left on a sawhorse, right at a kindergarten student's eye level. The student ran into the corner of the plywood while exiting the gym. Her injury required several stitches. Janice spent a good deal of time with the student's parents explaining the safety precautions that were being taken. She wrote a letter of apology. She held parent meetings and staff meetings. She felt like she was always apologizing for the actions of others and the state of her school. She decided to spend even more time doing safety checks throughout the school, and she met with the construction foreman daily. She couldn't wait for the construction project to be finished.

Discussion Questions

* Was the principal responsible for the actions of the construction workers?
* Who is responsible for the safety of students on a construction site?
* What role could the school's Occupational Health and Safety Committee have played in this situation?

* What role should the school district play when a school is under construction?

4

HORMONES OR HARASSMENT?

On September 14 at 6:30 p.m., just one week after the students had returned to classes, Principal Janice Wright received a phone call at home. It was the mother of a girl in grade 7. She was very concerned about some things that had apparently being said at school to her daughter Amy and to Amy's friend Alison by their classmate Nicole. Amy's mother said that the things that Nicole was saying were so inappropriate that they warranted an expulsion from school. In fact, Amy's mother wanted Janice to expel Nicole immediately.

Janice told Amy's mother that this was the first she had heard of this problem and that she would look into it the next day at school. She asked Amy's mother why she had contacted her at home. She explained that her daughter was very upset, and she wanted to deal with it immediately. Janice replied that she was not prepared to do anything until the following day at school. Amy's mother then asked Janice not to speak to her daughter about the problem unless she, the mother, was present.

Ten minutes later, the phone rang again. This time it was Alison's father. He told Janice that Alison was at home in tears because of what was happening at school. He said that Nicole was saying rude and inappropriate things of a sexual nature about his daughter. He told Janice that he wanted this behaviour to stop immediately or he would involve his lawyers. Janice explained to him that she had not been aware that there was a problem. It had not been reported to her by either of the girls, their teacher, or the playground supervisors. Janice told Alison's dad that she would look into it the next day at school. She also asked him to contact her at school and not at home, unless it was an emergency. He apologized, but he felt that this problem warranted a call to Janice at home. He then went on to explain that the three girls had been friends but over the summer they had had a falling out. Consequently, there were now bad feelings between the girls. Alison's father was upset about this since Nicole had spent a considerable amount of time at their house over the summer, and the girls had been very close. He said that Nicole was now no longer welcome in their home. He wanted Nicole to be expelled from the school so that his daughter would not have to deal with this harassment any longer.

The next day, Janice spoke to the girls' teacher, Ms. Bright. She was not aware of any problems between the girls. She had not seen any of the girls in tears or visibly upset in any way at school. She was quite surprised at what Amy and Alison claimed Nicole had said.

Janice then spoke to Nicole. She asked Nicole if there were any problems between her and any other girls in her class. Nicole replied that she was not getting along very well with Amy and Alison and that they were talking about her and saying mean things about her to the other grade 7 girls. She said that they were making her feel uncomfortable. Janice told her the things that Amy and Alison said Nicole was saying about them. Nicole flatly denied having said anything of that nature.

Janice then spoke to Alison. Alison explained that the problems she was having with Nicole arose from several incidents that had happened over the summer. She just wanted things to stop. Her solution, like her parents', was to send Nicole away from the school. Janice told her that this was neither a solution nor an option. Janice suggested that things needed to be worked out through discussion and problem-solving strategies, perhaps involving the school counsellor. Alison was agreeable to this. Both Alison and Nicole were told that they needed to report any incidents to their teacher or to Janice as soon as they happened so that they could be dealt with immediately.

Janice then spoke to the two grade 7 teachers. Because Amy, Alison, and Nicole were all in the same class, they decided that they would move Nicole into the other class. This would limit interactions between Nicole and the other two girls and help reduce their discomfort with each other. Nicole was consulted about this, and she seemed relieved and satisfied with this solution. Janice made several attempts to contact Nicole's mother to talk to her about what was going on. She left messages on the answering machine and sent a note home about Nicole's class change. It was evident that Nicole did not have the parental support that Amy and Alison enjoyed.

Discussion Questions

* When is it appropriate for parents to call the principal at home?
* Where does the administrator's responsibility end with respect to student behaviour off the school grounds?
* What policies should be in place regarding the bullying behaviours of name-calling and exclusion? Should students be involved in setting these policies?

See appendix, page 129

5

EMERGENCY PROCEDURES

In early September, Principal Janice Wright received a phone call from the fire chief. He told her that Jake Mantel, a teacher on her staff, was a member of the city's volunteer fire department. The fire chief explained to Janice that the city relied on its volunteers, especially in the event of a major fire or accident. He asked Janice if she would give her permission to release Jake from his teaching duties in the event of a major fire or accident. He said that he made this call routinely to all of the volunteers' supervisors and that usually he had not had a problem obtaining this permission. Janice explained to the fire chief that in this case there would be a problem since Mr. Mantel was a teacher and would be unable to leave his students. She said that she had to put her students' safety first and that it would be impossible for Mr. Mantel to leave them unattended to go and fight a fire. She could not assure coverage for Mr. Mantel as she herself was teaching 20 per cent of the school day and was not always in the school. She asked the fire chief if there were other teachers on the volunteer brigade. He replied that there were no other teachers and said that he could understand her concerns. He thanked Janice for her time.

Later that day, Janice met with Mr. Mantel and told him about her conversation with the fire chief. Mr. Mantel seemed to understand and agreed that he could not leave his class unattended to go to fight a fire.

At lunch hour one day near the end of October, the school secretary, Mrs. James, received a phone call. It was Mr. Mantel. He told her that just before lunch a major fire had broken out in a residential area. Because it was his lunch hour, he had decided to go and help. Lunch hour was now almost over, but it looked as though he would not be able to make it back to the school. The fire was a bad one, and they needed him there. He asked Mrs. James to find someone to cover for him. He told her that he would call her back in a few minutes. He did not ask to speak to Janice. Mrs. James found Janice and told her what had happened. Janice was not impressed. She had a grade 2 class to teach that afternoon. The librarian did not work that day so she could not cover Mr. Mantel's class either. It was too late to call in a substitute teacher. It looked as though Janice would have to look after Mr. Mantel's grade sevens and her grade twos. What choice did she have? Janice told Mrs. James that if Mr. Mantel called back, she wanted to speak to him.

Ten minutes into the afternoon session, Mr. Mantel called, and Mrs. James brought Janice the portable phone. Janice asked Mr. Mantel if there was anyone in danger of losing their life at the fire. Mr. Mantel replied that the occupants of the house had not been at home when the fire started and that everyone was safe, but they were in danger of losing the house. Janice directed Mr. Mantel to return to the school immediately.

Mr. Mantel returned to the school and resumed his duties in the classroom. He left the school as soon as the dismissal bell rang and returned to the fire.

Discussion Questions

* Could or should the principal have handled this situation differently?
* Are there situations where it would be appropriate for a teacher to leave his or her teaching duties and leave students unsupervised?

See appendix, page 130

6

THE EMAILED COMPLAINT

It was October, and the school year was underway at last. Things were quiet one morning, so Principal Janice Wright sat down to read her email. She scanned her inbox and noticed that there was an email from a name she did not recognize. What she did recognize, however, was the teacher's name in the subject line. Janice quickly scrolled down to the item and opened it. The letter was from Mrs. Black, a parent well known in the school. In the email, she alleged that the grade 3 teacher, Mr. Tate, had grabbed her daughter's chin in order to make her listen. She also wrote that, out of frustration and anger, Mr. Tate constantly yelled at the students and that he had, on several occasions, thrown items across the room. Mrs. Black claimed that she had spoken to many other parents, and they were all concerned about Mr. Tate's ability to handle the classroom. Further, she alleged that she had told Janice of her concerns on several occasions but that Janice had not done a thing. Mrs. Black had sent a copy of the email to the superintendent of schools.

Janice knew that she had to respond to the allegations in the letter. As she was thinking about how best to do this, the phone rang. It was the superintendent. He wanted to know what she was doing about the letter from Mrs. Black. Janice told him that this parent disliked Mr. Tate, and she was not so sure that anything untoward had taken place. She explained that she felt that Mr. Tate was a competent teacher, although there had been several allegations about Mr. Tate yelling at children. They discussed the contents of the email, and the superintendent told Janice that because there was an allegation of a child being grabbed, she needed to make a formal investigation. He added that he would phone Mrs. Black to tell her that Janice would be investigating the allegations made in the letter.

Discussion Questions

* Should Janice give Mr. Tate a copy of the email that was sent to her and the superintendent?
* In terms of privacy, is an email letter different from a letter received through the post?
* When does yelling to control a class become a problem to be investigated? How can an administrator help a teacher who yells at the class to get the students' attention?
* If a complaint against a teacher is found to be invalid, should a copy of the complaint and the results of the investigation be placed in the teacher's file?
* When a parent has made a complaint about a teacher and it has resulted in an investigation of the teacher's behaviour, does the parent have a right to know about the process and the results of the investigation?

See appendix, page 131

7

THE REALITY OF ADD

———·+·———

Jeff Edwards, a grade 5 teacher at Harmony Elementary, had a reputation in the community for being an excellent teacher. He worked extremely hard and set high standards for himself and his students. He coached basketball, volleyball, and track. He went on a major trip with his class every year. He provided his students with rich and challenging experiences. This year, Mr. Edwards had a large and fairly difficult class. However, it was a straight grade 5 class, not a grade 5–6 split, like he had the year before.

One of the boys in Mr. Edwards's class was particularly challenging for him. Kyle had trouble staying in his seat. He was also disorganized and not very good at reading. He could never find his pencils, pens, or notebooks. He constantly played with things in his desk, taking apart pens, breaking erasers into tiny pieces, and breaking pencils in half. Kyle's handwriting was nearly illegible. In fact, Kyle was unable to use cursive writing. All of his work was printed and looked like it had been done by a grade 2 student. Kyle had been at the school for two years and during these two years had spent a fair amount of time with the special education teacher. He was on an individualized education program (IEP).

At a meeting at the beginning of the school year, Mr. Edwards had been told by the special education teacher and by Kyle's parents that Kyle had attention deficit disorder and although Kyle had above-average intelligence, he would not be able to complete written tasks in the same way as other students. He would also be unable to sit and work at his desk for long periods of time. At this meeting, strategies for dealing with Kyle's needs had been discussed extensively. The program of study would have to be adapted for Kyle, especially with regard to written output. The special education teacher said that she would like to continue to work with Kyle on a regular basis, for thirty minutes every morning. Kyle's parents were very supportive and very knowledgeable about Kyle's special needs. Kyle's mother was a teacher at another school.

Mr. Edwards had left the meeting feeling overwhelmed. He was concerned that Kyle would not do well in his academically challenging program. He was also concerned about the amount of time Kyle would be out of his classroom each day. How was he going to bring Kyle up to speed when he returned to the classroom? And why should he have to change his expectations for written assignments? If Kyle had above-average intelligence, he should be able to complete the work, just like any other student.

As the month of September progressed, Mr. Edwards realized that Kyle was not just any other student. Mr. Edwards was becoming increasingly frustrated with Kyle. He seemed to be constantly out of his seat, either talking to other students or at the pencil sharpener. He took a long time to copy things from the board, and his reading was very poor. In addition to all this, it seemed to Mr. Edwards that Kyle was not making a very good effort to keep up with the work he missed while he was out working with the special education teacher. Mr. Edwards was more than a little suspicious about what the special education teacher was doing with Kyle. He often saw them in the gym shooting baskets or outside running or kicking a soccer ball around the field. Why was he out playing while he should be in the class working like all the other students? Kyle often went home with a lot of homework—work he was unable to finish in class.

At the beginning of October, Principal Janice Wright received a call from Kyle's mother. She said that she was feeling frustrated with what was happening with her son in Mr. Edwards' class.

Kyle was very unhappy and uptight. He was spending four hours each night on homework assignments. He was petrified of Mr. Edwards and was trying very hard to make all of his work perfect for him. He had even asked her to tape the alphabet in cursive writing onto his desk so that he could carefully copy each letter in all of his written work. She asked Janice to attend a meeting with her, her husband, and Mr. Edwards. Janice asked Kyle's mother if they had tried to speak with Mr. Edwards before asking her to participate. She assured her that they had, several times, and that many problems remained unresolved.

Janice went to speak to Mr. Edwards to get his take on the situation. He seemed to bristle at the mention of Kyle's name. He commented that Kyle's mother was being quite pushy, phoning and writing notes in Kyle's agenda to tell him how many hours Kyle had spent doing homework the previous night. Mr. Edwards explained to Janice that on several occasions, Kyle's mother, who said that she was simply acting as Kyle's scribe, had written Kyle's reading comprehension homework. Mr. Edwards also told how one day he had taken it upon himself to make written observations of Kyle's activities over the course of an entire morning. He then sent these home to Kyle's parents so that they could see exactly what he had to deal with each day. Mr. Edwards said that Kyle's parents had not even thanked him for doing this; they had simply made more requests for Mr. Edwards to adapt his programs and expectations to meet Kyle's needs.

Janice arranged the meeting between herself, Mr. Edwards, the special education teacher, and Kyle's parents. Prior to the meeting, the special education teacher again went over Kyle's IEP with Mr. Edwards. Janice was in attendance at this session. At this meeting, the special education teacher mentioned how much she enjoyed working with Kyle, that he was co-operative and very much wanted to please his teachers. Janice noted that many adaptations had been recommended in the IEP. She also noted that Mr. Edwards was not really buying into the program. He had many excuses for why he was not following the recommendations.

It was also clear to Janice that Mr. Edwards was very resentful that he was being asked to change the way he did things for one student and that he didn't seem to like Kyle very much. Janice was apprehensive about the meeting with Kyle's parents.

Mr. Edwards began the meeting by telling Kyle's parents how hard he had to work in order to get Kyle to do things properly. He continued by saying that he felt that Kyle was taking up too much of his time at the expense of the other students in his class. Kyle's parents said that Kyle worked very hard at home and that it was really important to him that his work was up to Mr. Edwards' standards. They also said that Kyle spent a lot of time worrying about whether or not his work was good enough for Mr. Edwards. He often ripped work up and started over. At home, he was often frustrated and in tears, and he was having trouble sleeping. A few days ago, Kyle had said that he knew that Mr. Edwards didn't like him, no matter how hard he tried. They had brought a book about dealing with students with attention deficit disorder to the meeting for Mr. Edwards to read. Kyle's mother said that the book had been really helpful to her as a teacher and as a parent. At that point, Mr. Edwards pushed the book back towards Kyle's mother and stood up. He said that he did not need advice from another teacher about how to teach and that he did not believe in ADD. With that, he left the room. The special education teacher excused herself. Janice was left with Kyle's parents. She apologized for Mr. Edwards' behaviour. Kyle's parents were visibly upset. Janice tried to assure them that things would change in the class and that Kyle's needs would be met. There was no possibility of moving Kyle to another class, since this was the only grade 5 class in the school. Kyle's parents said that they would speak to her the next day because they needed some time to think.

Discussion Questions

* What recourse does the principal have if a teacher does not follow an individualized education plan?

- How should the principal deal with the teacher's behaviour at the meeting?
- Should a parent be treated differently because he or she is a teacher? Why or why not?

See appendix, page 132

8

WHEN A PARENT MISBEHAVES

Although it was after school on a Thursday, many students were still in the school. Some had band practice, and others had tutoring. The band teacher had let the band out early, so Justin decided to wait in the computer lab for his sister until she was finished her tutoring next door in the learning centre. He placed his saxophone outside the computer lab so that his sister would see it when she came out.

Carolyn, a special education assistant and a parent of a student at Harmony Elementary, was waiting in the hallway for her daughter, who was also being tutored. As she waited, she watched Dawn, a new parent in the school, approach, holding the hand of her grade 1 child. Dawn stopped outside the computer lab, picked up the saxophone, and continued down the hall. Carolyn was puzzled. She knew that Dawn's daughter was not old enough to be in the band. Because she worked in the school, Carolyn also knew that Dawn was not the best of parents. Almost every day her daughter, Jade, came to school late. She rarely had a lunch, and some questionable-looking people often picked her up after school. Carolyn knew that last week the school administration had spoken to Dawn about whom they should allow Jade to go home with. There was a rumour that Dawn was heavily involved in drugs.

Carolyn was quite sure that the saxophone did not belong to Dawn. She didn't know what to do. She did not want to confront Dawn. She had seen Dawn in action at the office last week. Dawn had been confrontational and verbally abusive. Carolyn decided to follow Dawn to see what she was going to do with the saxophone.

Dawn exited the school and began walking towards the main street, pulling Jade along with one hand and clutching the saxophone case with the other. Carolyn kept a safe distance. She felt a little like a private detective. Dawn had no idea she was being followed as she walked right into a pawnshop. Carolyn watched from the other side of the street as Dawn exited, one hand still holding Jade's, and the other hand empty. Dawn and Jade continued walking, and Carolyn ran back to the school, just in time to pick up her own daughter. By this time, there was quite a commotion going on in the hallway outside the computer lab. Justin was in tears, explaining to the principal, Janice Wright, that his saxophone had disappeared. Carolyn pulled Janice aside and told her what she had just witnessed. Janice thanked Carolyn for her great detective work. She told Justin that she would take care of the saxophone problem and said that he and his sister could go home. She would phone their parents later that evening. She then phoned the police.

A detective arrived at the school a few minutes later. She got a statement from Carolyn and proceeded to the pawnshop. The saxophone was still there. The detective interviewed the pawnshop clerk and retrieved the saxophone. The detective asked Janice if she wanted to press charges. Janice did not want to do anything that might have a negative impact on Jade. She was worried that if she upset things, Dawn might be jailed or might flee to another town and move her daughter yet again. However, she also had to think of the safety of all the students in her school, and she did not want to have to follow Dawn whenever she came into the school. Janice asked the detective if it would be possible to get a restraining order against Dawn that would restrict her from entering the school grounds. If this were possible, Jade could still attend the school and have some stability in her life. The detective said that a restraining order would be a good option and that she would go over to Dawn's house to bring her in for questioning.

Discussion Questions

* Should Janice have called the police?
* What are the school's options when a parent does something unlawful or becomes violent on school property?

See appendix, page 132

9

REPORT CARD DILEMMAS

———·+·——

After the first term reports were sent home, Principal Janice Wright met with a parent, at the parent's request. The parent was dissatisfied with her daughter's English mark. Ivy, a grade 4 student, had received a C+. Her mother said that she was not satisfied with the mark and wanted it changed. She felt that her daughter was better than a C+ student. She felt that Ivy was an A student. She then went on to explain that their family was going to be moving to another city and that she was trying to enrol Ivy in a private school. Apparently the school would not accept students with Cs on their report cards.

Janice explained to the Ivy's mother that her teacher had assigned the mark on her report card and that it was the teacher's professional judgement she was questioning. Janice asked her if she had spoken to Mrs. Chen, Ivy's teacher, about this. She said that she had and that Mrs. Chen had refused to change the mark. Ivy's mother said that she would come back to see Janice in a week's time to discuss the matter further. Janice said that she would look into the matter in the meantime.

Janice then went to see Mrs. Chen, a teacher with twenty years' experience. Mrs. Chen explained that after meeting with the parent, she had reviewed Ivy's work and her mark. She was not prepared to change the mark. It reflected what Ivy was able to do. She asked Janice if she would look at Ivy's portfolio and give her opinion. Janice agreed. After examining it, Janice concluded that Ivy's was definitely C work. She felt that Mrs.Chen had been generous when she gave Ivy a C+. She met with Mrs. Chen and shared her opinion. Mrs. Chen explained that Ivy was involved in figure skating and that she often handed assignments in late because she was so busy with her skating. She was also frequently absent or late because of her skating commitments. When Janice had examined Ivy's work, it was evident to her that many of the assignments had been completed in a rush. Mrs. Chen explained that she gave extra time to Ivy to complete her assignments and that she had made many concessions for her. However, there was no improvement in the quality of Ivy's work.

Janice again met with Ivy's mother, who asked Janice if the mark would be changed. Janice explained to her that she had spoken with Mrs. Chen, and, at the teacher's request, had spent some time examining Ivy's work. She told Ivy's mother that she fully supported Mrs. Chen's professional judgement. The mark would remain a C+. She also explained that a C+ is a satisfactory mark. Ivy's mother, however, was not satisfied. She said that Ivy's teacher should have warned her that improvement was needed before sending out the report. Janice asked her if she had attended the parent-teacher conferences last month. She had not. They had been away skating.

Ivy's mother was not happy with Janice's decision not to change the mark. She blamed Mrs. Chen for Ivy's "poor" mark. She stated that Mrs. Chen should have communicated the homework assignments directly to her. Janice explained that Mrs. Chen had communicated with her on a regular basis through Ivy's agenda and weekly reports. Janice explained that students were expected to fill out their agenda and the parents were expected to check and initial them every night. Ivy's mother had not been doing this. She replied that Ivy often came home without any homework. Janice told her that she thought this was rather odd, because, according to Mrs. Chen, Ivy was three weeks behind in her work and, in fact, Ivy's mother had been told this by Mrs. Chen when they had met the week before. Janice also told Ivy's mother that she had a responsibility to contact the teacher about work that Ivy had missed because of skating.

Ivy's mother was fuming. She argued that Ivy's C+ was the

school's fault. She expected nothing but As from her daughter, and she wanted to be informed by the school any time that Ivy was performing below an A. Janice told her that she needed to understand that an A was only given for outstanding work. She questioned whether she was putting undue stress on her child with these high expectations. Ivy was in grade 4. This was the first year she had received letter grades. How did she know that Ivy was an A student? Janice explained that students are always encouraged to do their best at the school. Ivy's mother questioned this; in fact, she felt that students should always have the opportunity to redo their work until it is A work. Janice replied that it would be difficult for this to happen with all assignments because the teacher would never get through the curriculum. Janice also explained that she, as a parent, was a partner with the school and that she had a responsibility to support the school and her child by checking Ivy's agenda and contacting the teacher for missed work when Ivy was absent. Ivy's mother left Janice's office in a huff. She threatened to call the superintendent.

Discussion Questions

* Do parents have the right to appeal a letter grade?
* What appeal processes have you encountered in schools where you have worked, and how have these processes been communicated to the parents?
* When reviewing an appeal, what are the key issues that an administrator should address?
* What is the administrator's role in the assignment of marks?

See appendix, page 133

10

HANDS OFF!

———•+•———

It was the evening of the parent-teacher conferences. Principal Janice Wright was working at her desk when two parents entered her office. Before they even introduced themselves, the father demanded to know why the school had a hands-off rule. He appeared to be quite agitated.

Janice did not recognize these parents. She asked them whose parents they were and invited them to sit down. They replied that they were Kevin Hamel's parents. Kevin, a boy in grade 5, was not a regular visitor to Janice's office, but she had dealt with him and several other grade 5 boys a few weeks earlier.

Janice had met twice with the boys and reminded them about the school's hands-off rule after teachers on duty at recess and lunch hour supervisors had warned them not to play so roughly. The first time, she gave them a warning, but the problem did not go away. The second time, each boy had filled out a behaviour-report form, taken it home to be signed by a parent, and returned it to the school. A few days later, Kevin and another boy had been brought into the office by one of the teachers on recess duty. She said that they had been fighting. Kevin had denied this, but the teacher said that she had seen him kick the other boy and then "go at him." There was no doubt in her mind that these boys had been fighting. Janice had spoken very sternly to the boys and told them both that any further violation of the hands-off rule would result in a suspension. The boys had assured her that they would change their ways. After discussing the problem with Janice, the teacher had taken them outside and shown them how to play flag football and other non-violent games. This seemed to help. Janice had not had to deal with them again. She was surprised to see these parents in her office, as there had been no more problems with their son.

After listening to Janice's explanation of the hands-off rule, Mr. and Mrs. Hamel then referred to the most recent fighting incident. They said that Kevin had been falsely accused of fighting. He had only been defending himself. Janice said that, from the teacher's account of the incident and the discussion that they had had with Kevin afterwards, there was no question that Kevin had indeed been fighting.

A discussion then ensued about how students should defend themselves. Kevin's parents said that they had told their son to fight back. Janice described the conflict-resolution and anti-bullying programs that were in place in the school to provide students with excellent alternatives to getting physical. Mr. and Mrs. Hamel continued to defend their views for another twenty-five minutes. Mr. Hamel was becoming more and more aggressive and confrontational, saying things like:

> "The last principal had a designated area for snowballs and rough play"(Janice knew that this was not true.);
>
> "You are running a boot camp here";
>
> "Do you watch sports on television? There is a lot of physical contact, and people don't freak out about it. No, I bet you only watch golf";
>
> "Your idea of a good time is probably reading a book. You can't possibly understand kids"; and
>
> "You will not suspend my son, even if he is caught breaking the hands-off rule!"

Janice had had enough. It was obvious that Kevin's parents were being irrational. She was being personally attacked, even though she reminded the parents that it was not about her. She was becoming a little worried about her safety. There was no one else in the office, Mr. Hamel smelled of alcohol, and Mrs. Hamel was yelling along with him; it was time to call the meeting to an end. She told the Hamels that the meeting was over and that they were welcome to make an appointment to see her and the vice-principal on another day. Mr. Hamel replied that he was going to take his concerns to the superintendent. Janice encouraged them to do so, and she told them that the school district did not condone rough play or physical retaliation. Swearing, Kevin's parents stormed out of her office. Janice, shaken, returned to her desk.

Discussion Questions

* What are the benefits of a hands-off policy?
  What recourse do parents have when they do not agree with a school policy?
* What recourse does an administrator have when confronted with insults and verbal abuse from disgruntled parents?
* How could the principal educate the parent committee about the hands-off policy?

See appendix, page 133

11

PARENT HELPERS?

———•—•———

As Principal Janice Wright entered the school office shortly before the bell rang to signal the beginning of the lunch hour, she overheard the secretary and a prep teacher discussing the actions of one of the parent helpers. She could tell by the tone of their voices that something they didn't like had taken place. When they saw her enter the office, they both approached her and said, almost in unison, "You need to know what Ms. Fielding did today! She needs to be talked to!" With a sense of foreboding, Janice slowly put down the books she was carrying and asked what had happened.

Ms. Fielding had come in that day for her bimonthly parent-helper role in the grade 1 classroom. According the prep teacher, the teacher, Ms. Hatter, suspected that Ms. Fielding volunteered so that she could see how her daughter was progressing and check out the teaching methods. Ms. Hatter had grown so tired of her overbearing manner that she had resorted to giving her the "pencil-sharpening" jobs. Ms. Fielding had spent the first hour and a half of the morning doing mundane classroom jobs. After recess, the prep teacher asked Ms. Fielding back to help with the gymnastics stations in the gym. In light of the extra help, the prep teacher had redesigned what she was going to do in the gym. She developed a station that would require full-time adult supervision by Ms. Fielding. The prep teacher expected Ms. Fielding to stay at her assigned station.

But shortly after the students had been assigned to the stations,

Ms. Fielding left her station. When the prep teacher questioned her later about why she had left, Ms. Fielding told her what had happened and what she had done. She had noticed that there was a student who had started crying and holding his stomach. She figured that the teacher was much too busy to help with the child and so she left her station and took the child into the hallway to sit down in a chair. She asked him if he had felt sick earlier, and he replied that he had not. Ms. Fielding then decided to take him to the sickroom. As she was about to leave him there, she noticed that his pain seemed to get worse. She held him for a few minutes and, in her words, "I forcefully suggested that the secretary call his parents." Ms. Fielding retrieved his shoes from the gym and, upon learning that the secretary had not reached the parents, took it upon herself to phone them. She identified herself as being from the school and suggested that they come to the school and pick their son up and take him directly to the emergency ward of the hospital. She said that she had made this suggestion based on the fact that at one point, he had thrown up clear fluids. She then phoned the emergency ward, again identified herself as being from the school, and told them that she was sending in a seriously ill child. All of this had been done without the knowledge of the prep teacher or the school secretary.

Ms. Hatter had been in the staff room immediately adjacent to the office and the medical room, yet at no time was she consulted about any of the events that had transpired. The prep teacher told Janice that after she had listened to Ms. Fielding's version of the events, she spoke with her about the inappropriateness of parent helpers leaving an assigned area with a student without telling the teacher in charge.

After Janice heard the sequence of events from the prep teacher, she knew that she had to speak to Ms. Fielding as soon as possible. She walked to the classroom where she found Ms. Fielding madly scribbling down the details of the events. Janice asked her if she had ten minutes to come by her office so that they could talk. Ms. Fielding replied, "Well, I know I am in big trouble now, but I didn't do anything wrong." Janice assured her that she was not in trouble, but they did need to talk.

Five minutes later, Ms. Fielding entered Janice's office and said, "I've been sent to the principal's office. I'm in trouble. That's what all of the grade 1 students are saying. I am so embarrassed!" Janice once again assured her that this wasn't about "getting in trouble," but that they needed to clarify some school procedures. Janice then invited Ms. Fielding to tell her about what had happened. Her explanation of events was similar to the account given by the prep teacher and the secretary. Ms. Fielding explained that she felt the prep teacher was unconcerned about the child and that she could not have left the child to tell the prep teacher that there was a problem. She felt justified in leaving the gym with the child. She stated, "I couldn't wait for the teacher to take a break and finally notice that the child was sick."

Janice informed her that as a parent helper she was not to arbitrarily remove students from any class. Ms. Fielding replied, "Well, what should I do? Just let him lay there on the floor crying in pain until the teacher finally takes the time to do something?" Janice stated that it was the responsibility of the teacher and the school's first-aid officer to make determinations of illness or injury and, if warranted, to phone the parents. Upon hearing this, Ms. Fielding became very agitated and replied, "Well, the secretary let me do it. I did it here last year!" Janice acknowledged that this experience had certainly indicated to her that the school needed to have classroom volunteer orientations so that the roles and responsibilities of parent helpers could be better defined.

The following Wednesday evening was the Parent Advisory Council (PAC) meeting. Janice should have realized that something was brewing when Ms. Fielding appeared, for the first time, at the meeting. The meeting began at 7:30 p.m., and discussions around some old business carried on until about 9:00 p.m. At that time, Ms. Fielding said the words that any administrator dreads: "I have been talking to some other parents, and WE think that an incident that happened at the school needs to be brought to the attention of the PAC." She then handed a letter to Mrs. Wilson, the PAC president, and the other five faithful attendees. She did not hand one to Janice. Janice remarked that since this matter dealt with something that had happened at the school, she would have liked to have been informed that it was being brought forward at the meeting. Ms. Fielding replied, "Oh, I tried to reach you, but you are so hard to reach." She then read out the letter. It contained several inaccuracies. Janice pointed these out to the group. The discussion proceeded, and the meeting ended with Janice assuring the parents that she would share the letter with the staff and that they would discuss the concerns raised in the letter. That seemed to satisfy the PAC, but Ms. Fielding still appeared to be upset. She was heard mumbling, "She doesn't listen to anyone at this school."

Discussion Questions

* When are schools responsible for the actions of parent helpers?
* What kind of information would an effective handbook for parent volunteers contain?
* Does a parent have the right to bring an issue up at a PAC meeting without the PAC president and/or principal's prior approval?
* How could all of this have been avoided?

See appendix, page 134

12

THE VICTIM

Vice-Principal Doug Simard had worked hard with Janice Wright, the principal, to change the "let boys be boys" attitude towards fighting and bullying that had been prevalent at the school. They had established fair, firm, and consistent consequences for bullying and fighting. They had been working with the staff to show them how to teach the students to respond to bullying behaviour appropriately. They had identified the provocative victims and encouraged those students to act in ways that were more acceptable to the other children. Annual bullying surveys had been done for the past two years. There had been presentations to the Parent Advisory Council on the topic of bullying. Doug had written several articles in the newsletter explaining what the school was doing and stressing the importance of teaching students strategies to deal with bullying. He felt confident that Harmony Elementary School was a safe place to be.

It was just before the Christmas holiday when Doug heard shrieking coming from outside. The snow was red when he arrived at the scene. Gilbert was clutching his nose, and Jason was shouting, "He threw an orange at me and called me names, so I hit him!"

Doug sent Gilbert to the medical room and brought Jason into the office. He agreed with Jason that students should not throw oranges at each other and that name-calling was not an appropriate thing to do, but hitting another student in the nose was unacceptable. Doug suspended Jason for two days. He then spoke to Gilbert, who admitted to throwing the orange and to name-calling. Since Gilbert was seldom in trouble, Doug spoke to him about his behaviour and left it at that. Both boys agreed that it would be a good idea if they stayed away from each other on the playground. When Gilbert's parents were informed of the incident, they were outraged by the violent behaviour of the other student. They told Doug that the school had not been safe since the former principal left.

In March there was another incident involving Gilbert and another boy named Darrell. Doug investigated the incident and determined that it was fairly minor in nature. However, to be on the safe side, he wrote the following letter to the parents:

Dear Parents of Gilbert Elleck and Darrell Burnside:

Today, your sons were involved in a fight at school. Evidently it started when Gilbert said that he was faster than Darrell. Some words were exchanged, then Darrell said he was stronger than Gilbert, and some more words were exchanged. This occurred just at the end of recess. When they returned to the classroom, Darrell pushed Gilbert's head onto his desk "to show that he was stronger." Gilbert retaliated by punching Darrell. Both boys were removed from the classroom. Darrell left the school to go to an eye appointment. Gilbert came down to the office to work in a quiet place. Ice was applied to his head. There was a slight red mark on his face from the push against the desktop. This afternoon, I had intended to have both boys sit down together and come up with a plan for getting along. Since Darrell did not return after his eye appointment, I would like to do this on Monday morning. If you have any questions or concerns, please phone me at the school.

Sincerely,

Mr. Simard

Doug locked up his office on Friday afternoon and left for the weekend. On Monday morning he received the following letter from Gilbert's father:

Dear Mr. Simard and staff,

After reading your letter about Gilbert and Darrell it appears to me that once again my child, Gilbert, was assaulted. I can't believe this is being allowed at school. I spoke to Gilbert on several occasions over the weekend, and the story I am getting is that he was attacked from behind, placed in a headlock, and his head was slammed repeatedly into the desktop. Gilbert was punching and elbowing Darrell to protect himself and get out of the headlock. Where I come from, this is assault. It is not acceptable and could have re-injured Gilbert's nose, which has not recovered from the last assault by Jason at your school. The consequences to Darrell, based on my past experience, will be nothing. If there are rules and regulations in place, they should be enforced. If this were done, I believe the school would be a safer place for all. However, if the situation is dealt with like the situation with Jason, and the students are simply instructed to avoid one another, these incidents will only become more regular in occurrence. The students need some leadership and accountability for their actions. The school district and its employees are in that position during the school day. I see no accountability, which means that students get away with whatever they please. I, myself, am not sure how to deal with this, but I am concerned for my children's safety. In January of this year, after Jason's assault on Gilbert, I instructed all of my children that they have the right to protect themselves. I believe this is one of those situations where Gilbert was justified in defending himself. I believe that you and your staff have to take control of the situation rather than avoid the issue as you are doing. I have taken the liberty of sending this letter to my uncle who is on the school board. I phoned him about the problems at the school, and he said he would be phoning you.

Sincerely,

Mr. and Mrs. Peter Elleck

Discussion Questions

- What is the role of the school in teaching social responsibility and social skills to the students?
- What more could the school do to prevent bullying?
- What can the administrator do when the parents react only to the "victim's" version of the story?
- How should the school inform the parents of the school policy on bullying?

See appendix, page 134

13

APPROPRIATE SCHOOL CLOTHING

It was a Monday morning, and Vice-Principal Doug Simard was finally able to look at some of the mail that had piled up on his desk. As he was reaching the end of the mail, Ms. Hatter, the grade 1 teacher, entered his office and asked him, "Do you think children should wear underwear to school?" He looked at her to see if she was joking, but she appeared to be very concerned. He was also aware of a small boy standing just outside his office. Doug rightly assumed that this young man had prompted her question. It seems that Karl had not worn any underwear to school and that he had pulled his pants down to "moon" his favourite pals. Doug asked Karl to sit in the foyer of the office while he spoke to his teacher. He understood that he, as the vice-principal, would need to speak to Karl about the fact that he had pulled his pants down; however he was still a little unclear on the underwear issue. Ms. Hatter wanted to phone Karl's mother to speak to her about the need for her son to wear underwear to school. Doug suggested that maybe Karl had simply forgotten to put on his underwear or that perhaps Karl's parents did not think that underwear was an important item of clothing. However, Ms. Hatter was not to be dissuaded, and she went to contact the mother.

Meanwhile, Doug spoke to Karl. Karl said that he did not pull his pants down all the way—"just part way." Doug explained to him that this was an inappropriate behaviour at school. When he asked Karl about the underwear issue, he readily explained that when he was at his dad's house and had underwear on, his brother would give him painful "wedgies." Doug was aware that Karl had been at his dad's house on the weekend, so the explanation made sense.

Doug was away from the school at a principals' meeting on the following Thursday when Karl and Ms. Hatter had another problem. Karl had come back to the classroom after lunch and had been dancing around, saying, "I have to go to the bathroom," in a babyish voice. Ms. Hatter heard him but assumed that he was just fooling around. Karl continued with this behaviour until Ms. Hatter told him, "quit being silly and join the circle." He complied and, after a few minutes, asked to go to the bathroom. He was given permission. Ms. Hatter later realized that Karl had been gone a very long time, so she left the class and went to find him. He was still in the bathroom, but he had not made it in time. Ms. Hatter was unsure of what to do, but she gave him some moist towelettes and instructed him to clean himself up while she went to get a plastic bag for the soiled items. She also asked Mrs. James, the secretary, to phone Karl's parents to ask for some clean clothes to be brought to the school.

When Karl's mother got to the school with the clean clothes and heard what had happened, she became very angry about the whole incident and began yelling at Ms. Hatter about her lack of consideration and care. She took Karl home and vowed, "This is not the end of it!"

Doug arrived back at the school on Friday morning to find a note that said he had an appointment with Karl's mother and father on Monday morning. He sought out Ms. Hatter to find out what was going on. She explained what had happened and showed him the notes she had made after the incident.

Monday morning arrived, and Karl's mother and father were at the school. Doug asked them to come into his office and to sit down. They explained their unhappiness with Ms. Hatter. In addition to the bathroom incident, they listed the following concerns:

- Ms. Hatter had cut Karl's nails and then scrubbed his nails and hands with a nail brush because she said he had "dirty hands";
- Ms. Hatter had called them five times about Karl's "uncleanliness";
- They did not understand the school's concern about children wearing underwear at all times;
- Ms. Hatter had taken candy away from Karl and humiliated him about having it in his lunch. She did not give the candy back; and
- Ms. Hatter acted like she did like not their son.

Discussion Questions

- What is the school's role in determining appropriate hygiene and nutritional expectations?
- What is an appropriate dress code for students? How specific does it have to be?
- When should a principal formally investigate a teacher based on concerns reported by parents?

See appendix, page 134

14

DIABETES DILEMMA

———·—·———

Mattie Roberts and her parents were waiting patiently outside Principal Janice Wright's office. They had just moved to the neighbourhood and wanted to enrol Mattie in grade 2 at Harmony Elementary School. After Janice had finished her meeting with Vice-Principal Doug Simard regarding the upcoming assembly, she walked into the office foyer and greeted the Roberts family. Mrs. James, the school secretary, told her that Mr. and Mrs. Roberts had just filled out the registration forms for Mattie and she had consulted her class size chart determined that and there was room at Harmony Elementary School for a student in either of the grade 2 classes. Since this was all good news, Janice wondered why Mattie's parents looked so anxious and why they wanted to talk to her. She invited them into her office and closed the door.

Mrs. Robert explained that one year ago, Mattie had been very ill and was diagnosed with diabetes. She required insulin injections twice a day. Mrs. Roberts had home-schooled Mattie for the previous year, but she had found a job and was no longer able to home-school her daughter. Mr. and Mrs. Roberts were anxious to hear from Janice as to how students with diabetes were looked after at Harmony Elementary School. Janice was honest and said that they had never had a diabetic child at the school but that she would get in touch with the nursing support team from the local health unit. The assigned nurse would meet with Mr. and Mrs. Roberts and the school to finalize a medical care plan for Mattie.

Until that plan was in place and everyone was trained, Mattie could not start school. While the Robertses were not happy with the delayed start for Mattie, they understood the need to meet to develop a plan to ensure that everyone was properly trained.

Janice got in touch with the nursing support team, and a nurse was able to come to the school later that week. She contacted Mattie's parents and told them the date and time for the meeting. Janice had thought about who the best people at Harmony Elementary would be to train to look after Mattie's needs. She decided to place Mattie in a grade 2 class that had a student support worker in the classroom. Although the student support worker was there to support another student, this student did not need her all of the time. Janice also decided that the teacher, another student support worker, and she should also be trained in the medical care plan for Mattie.

The grade 2 student support worker was reluctant to be part of the team to support Mattie because she did not like needles. Janice assured her that she would not be giving the injection, just supervising the insulin injection, as agreed to in the care plan. The support worker grudgingly agreed to be trained, but only after she had checked with her union to see if supervising insulin injections was part of her job description. The union said that her job description did not specifically state anything about diabetes, but that it did say that the job was to do what was needed to support the assigned students, as requested by the principal. Both the teacher and Janice were willing to be trained, but the other support worker, who would be the back-up person in case the first support worker was away, was also reluctant. Janice ended up directing her to take the training.

The meeting was arranged, and everyone attended. Susan Carlson, the nurse, had developed the care plan and went over it with Mr. and Mrs. Roberts and the school personnel. Everyone signed off on the plan, and Mattie started school the following Monday. Susan came back in two weeks to see how the plan was working and met with the two student support workers. Both support workers told her that looking after Mattie and her needs made them nervous because her blood sugar levels fluctuated so much. Susan assured them that it was common in a diabetic student who was Mattie's age. As Susan was leaving, she reiterated the importance of sticking to the plan by stating, "You must follow this plan to the letter. Failure to do so will be a career-ending move and will result in legal action if anything should happen to Mattie."

Janice was not at that meeting with Susan and the two student support workers and was not aware of what had been said. She was surprised when she received a letter the next day, signed by both the support workers stating that they refused to supervise Mattie because they did not feel safe doing so. Janice talked to both of the support workers about what Susan had said and then she directed them to continue to supervise Mattie and follow the care plan. They did as they were told, but they filed a grievance with their union.

Discussion Questions

* What is the responsibility of the school to meet the needs of students who need medical procedures at school?
* Was Susan correct in what she said to the two student support workers about liability?

15

DUTY OF CARE

———•—

Vice-principal Doug Simard had just put the phone down in his office when he heard the sound of running feet in the hallway. He left his office and looked out into an empty hallway. He heard the outside door close and looked outside in time to see Darren Hoople, one of the students from the special needs class, standing at the front of the school. As Doug started out the door, the student ran away from him and across two lanes of traffic. Doug was not sure what to do, but knew something had to be done to ensure Darren's safety. He decided to call out to Darren and invite him back to the school. To his surprise, Darren started back across the street, once again dodging traffic. As Darren approached, he started shouting, "I never want to go to school here again! I hate this school! I want to get hit by a car!" As Doug was walking towards him to try to calm him, Darren turned and bolted into traffic again. This time, Doug took off after him to see if he could talk to Darren and somehow keep him safe. He was worried about being on a side of the school where no one could see him, and he did not have his cellphone with him. He was starting to wonder where the staff from the special needs class was. After he was able to approach and talk to Darren, Darren agreed to come back into the safety of the school but only if he could call his social worker. Doug thought this was reasonable given that the traffic was whizzing by and they had spent at least ten minutes talking on the median.

Doug and Darren returned to the school office and Doug

dialled the number of the social worker. She was not in, but Darren agreed to sit and wait in Doug's office. This gave Doug a chance to go to Darren's classroom. There he found the teacher, the school support worker, and the community support worker all talking about Darren's outburst and exit from the classroom. They had not moved. When Doug asked why no one had followed Darren, the community support worker replied that she had instructed the staff to let him go. She went on to say that this was the response that was ordered by the social worker based on information given to her by Darren's psychiatrist. Doug informed them that he had gone after Darren to ensure his safety and had talked him into coming into the school by promising him that he could phone his social worker. Upon hearing this, the school support worker and the community support worker both informed him that Darren was never, under any circumstances, to phone his social worker. The school support worker told Doug that by not following the agreed-upon protocol, he had created another set of problems with Darren. She went on to state, "Obviously you are well intentioned, but you really do not understand the nature of the needs of this type of child."

Doug asked the community support worker to show him the letter from the ministry instructing the school to let Darren run from the class and not to follow him. Doug remarked that he had not seen any communication of that sort in the file. He asked the teacher to bring him a copy of Darren's individualized education plan and demanded to know what strategies they had developed to keep Darren in class. Doug stated clearly that he expected Darren to be safe at all times. He explained that he understood that chasing after Darren could make him run without looking and could create a dangerous situation. However, they were expected to demonstrate a higher duty of care for the special needs students. Sitting at the other end of the school when a child had bolted from the room and was running into the street did not fulfil that expectation. By the time he was done his short speech, the teacher had located Darren's individualized education plan.

There were no documented strategies to deal with any behaviour related to running away from school.

Discussion Questions

* What should Doug do first? Why?
* What is the "duty of care" that is expected from staff members?
* Can an outside agency dictate school procedures?
* What are the liability issues associated with this scenario?

See appendix, page 135

16

A LITTLE TOLERANCE, PLEASE!

H armony Elementary, like its name, was usually a harmonious place to be. Students generally got along well. They felt safe, cared for, and respected at school. Harmony Elementary prided itself in its anti-bullying and conflict resolution programs. It took a proactive approach to these issues, and the approach seemed to be working.

One day, Principal Janice Wright received a call from the mother of a boy in grade 6. She said that she needed to see Janice as soon as possible. They made an appointment for that afternoon.

At the meeting, the parent, Mrs. Armir, expressed concern about her son Ross. Ross was an excellent student who loved coming to school. He was always positive and happy, but recently, Mrs. Armir had noticed a change in Ross's attitude. He seemed worried and preoccupied and sometimes quite negative about school. The day before, on the way home from school in the car, Ross had said something that was not at all typical: "James makes me so mad. I hope one day he gets tackled so hard in football that he never gets up." Ross had made this statement with a vehemence that alarmed his mother.

Later that night, Mrs. Armir and Ross had talked further about James. She found out that James, who was one of Ross's friends, had been making some upsetting comments to Ross. The Armir family was Muslim. This had never been an issue for Ross at school in the past, but recently, James had been making fun of Ross's religion. He had put his gym shorts on his head, put his hands together, and bowed several times in front of Ross. The group of boys that witnessed this had laughed, and so had Ross. Ross had said that it was sort of funny the first time. However, when James started doing this every time the class went to the gym, it stopped being funny to Ross and to most of the other boys, too. Then James had started calling Ross "Muslim boy" and making comments about how many times a day Ross and his family prayed. Ross was upset and felt that his friend had turned on him.

This had been going on for several weeks. Mrs. Armir was not aware of it until that day in the car. She was very upset. She told Janice that Ross did not know she was at school talking to her about the issue. Ross had indicated that he was reluctant to report it to his teacher or to the office. He was afraid the problem would become worse. He was afraid that James would find out and that all of the boys would turn against him. Janice explained that she wanted to investigate the concern and that she would need to speak with Ross in order to get all of the details. She also wanted to reassure Ross and offer him some advice for dealing with similar problems. She assured Mrs. Armir that there would be no repercussions for her son.

Janice was quite aware of who James was. He was a regular visitor at the office. In fact, earlier that week, she had received a phone call from a parent complaining about mean comments that James was making on the bus about her daughter. He had been ridiculing her about taking medication, calling her "mental." Janice had also spoken to James about comments he had made to some of the students in his class who went to learning assistance, saying that they were too stupid to do the work he was doing. Janice had worked hard with James, trying to help him to understand that the things he was saying were very hurtful. She had had him work as a peer helper with younger students. She had talked to him about his leadership qualities and how he could use them in positive ways that would benefit the school. They had even watched a movie together about how one boy had made an effort to go out of his way to be kind and the reverberating

positive effect this had had on those around him. James had re-
sponded well to Janice's interventions and always left the office
with good intentions. He just never seemed able to fulfill them.

James's mother was a single mom. She worked a lot at a job
that often required her to be away from home, and James was
left in the care of his uncle and aunt or his grandparents. James's
grandparents were from Greece and did not speak English, so
when there was a problem at school, there was often no follow-up
at home. Janice had tried several times to set up a meeting with
James's mother but had not been successful. His mother did not
return Janice's phone calls, and the letters she sent to his home
were returned signed by the grandparents or the uncle.

That afternoon, Janice and Vice-Principal Doug Simard met
with Ross. He told them what had been going on with James. He
said that he felt quite hurt about it because he and James had
been friends. Janice and Doug told Ross that the things James
was saying were not acceptable, even if James was only saying
them "as a joke." They explained that making fun of people or of
their beliefs did not contribute to a safe school environment. They
told Ross that they would be speaking to James about this. They
asked Ross to let them know if it happened again or if James said
or did anything that made Ross uncomfortable. Ross said that he
felt relieved that something was going to be done, and that, if possible, he wanted to remain friends with James

Next, Janice and Doug met with James. He admitted to having made fun of Ross on several occasions, but "only as a joke."
He said he did not know that he was upsetting Ross with his
comments. Again, Janice and Doug explained that making fun of
people or their beliefs was not acceptable behaviour at Harmony
Elementary. They reminded James of his previous visits to the
office for the hurtful comments he had made to other students.
James did not seem to be getting it. It was time to set up a meeting with James's mother. In the meantime, James told them that
he would stop making fun of his friend Ross.

After the meeting with James, Janice tried calling his mother. James had told her that his mother was not away and was

probably at home. However, nobody answered the phone. Janice left a message, asking her to phone the school as soon as possible. James's mother did not call back that day. The next day, Janice left two more messages. She finally called back one evening at 5:45 p.m., when Janice happened to be working late. James's mother, Sylvana, was abrupt and sounded angry. Janice explained the situation with Ross and recounted previous incidents when James had said unkind things. Sylvana's reaction surprised Janice. She said that Canadian people were too sensitive and that she had taught her son to "suck it up" when people said unkind things to him. She said that the school was being over-protective of its students and that the real world wasn't like that. Janice explained to her that what James was saying was making students feel unsafe and that James needed to stop. She said that she was looking for support from home, to help James understand the inappropriateness of his comments. Sylvana's reply went on for several minutes. She refused to acknowledge that James needed to change his behaviour. She refused to come in for a meeting to talk about how to support James and develop his potential in positive ways. She did not want to hear from the school again, unless her son was injured. She was too busy. With that, she hung up the phone. Now Janice had a better understanding of James. She wondered what she was going to do to support James and to help him become a better citizen.

Discussion Questions

* How should the school deal with a parent who does not support the school's philosophy and beliefs?
* How should the principal deal with a parent who refuses to attend a meeting?
* What policies should be in place in schools to deal with name-calling and mocking?
* Should the way that James was treating Ross be considered racist?

17

YOU BE THE PARENT

It was a quiet morning at Harmony Elementary School. The grade 4 to 7 classes were out of the building at a symphony concert. Janice Wright finally had time to observe in some of the kindergarten to grade 3 classrooms. She was just heading back to her office when Mrs. Lord approached and asked to speak to her. Mrs. Lord was Susan's, one of the girls in grade 7, grandmother and primary caregiver. Janice invited Mrs. Lord into her office to talk. Mrs. Lord wanted to know where her granddaughter was. Janice explained that they were at a concert and would be returning around eleven o'clock. Mrs. Lord continued to explain that she was looking for her Susan because she suspected that Susan was trading clothes with other students at school. Mrs. Lord then asked Janice if she had been paying any attention to how Susan had been dressing. Janice said she had not but that Susan must be falling within the bounds of the dress code or her teacher would have said something. Janice commented that Susan did seem to be trying on some different looks as she had noticed her wearing black lipstick on occasion. Upon hearing this, Mrs. Lord became angry, "What? Lipstick? She is not allowed to wear any makeup at home, and she should not be allowed to wear it at school." Mrs. Lord then asked, "What kind of school are you running here? Why do you people allow students to wear black lipstick?" She asked Janice if she could see where Susan's locker was located. Janice explained that it was in the main hallway, but if there was something that she needed to leave for Susan, she could leave it in the office. Mrs. Lord said that she would like Susan to put on the pair of sweatpants that she had brought because she was not going to be wearing any more of those "hipsters." Janice explained that she would give the pants to Susan, but she would not force to Susan put them on. Mrs. Lord was not happy with this response, but she was in a hurry. "Tell her she had better be wearing these when she gets home or else!"

Janice left the pants on the office counter and went into her office to answer phone messages. The students returned to the school at 11:40 a.m. Janice went to pick up the pants to give to Susan, but the pants were not on the counter. She then heard shouting in the hallway. One voice was Susan's, and the other unmistakable voice was her grandmother's. As Janice rounded the corner, she saw that Mrs. Lord and Susan were engaged in a heated argument. They were surrounded by five of Susan's friends. Mrs. Lord had a pair of "hipsters" in her left hand and was telling Susan that from now on, she was to only wear sweatpants. She went on to yell at Susan's friends and accused them of giving Susan inappropriate clothes and makeup to wear. Susan was in tears, and her friends were visibly upset. Janice walked up to them and told the girls to go to class. She asked Mrs. Lord to come to her office.

Once inside the principal's office, Mrs. Lord explained her actions by saying that she just wanted the best for her granddaughter. Janice told her that she could not have parents barging into the school, going through lockers, yelling at the students, and creating a scene. Mrs. Lord said that she felt justified because Janice was not willing to make Susan dress appropriately. Janice once again explained that she had very little control over how students were dressed at school unless it contravened the school dress policy. Mrs. Lord was not satisfied and demanded that Janice or Susan's teacher let her know whenever Susan was dressed in anything other than sweatpants or if she was wearing makeup at school. Janice again repeated that this was not something they were prepared to do. Mrs. Lord left, unhappy with the principal's decision.

Discussion Questions

* What rights do parents have to gain access to their child's locker?
* Should administrators and teachers act on requests from parents to police how students dress? Why or why not?
* How should an administrator deal with a parent who creates a scene in the hallway during school hours?
* How is the dress code decided? Who participates in dress code decisions? How should they be communicated to parents?

18

A MATTER OF POLICY

———•+•———

Basketball season had finally arrived. The grade 6–7 boys team eagerly swarmed around the coach as he explained about practices and upcoming games. The coach, Mr. Mantel, the grade 7 teacher, was happy with his team. The boys were keen, and most of them had good skills. He believed that they could become a strong team under his guidance and that this could be his school's year to get into the district finals, possibly even win the district championship. Three weekly practices were set up: two after school and one at lunch hour. There were three other school teams vying for prime gym time, so the gym schedule was tight.

The first two practices went smoothly. The boys were showing up on time and were eager to learn new basketball skills. Already, the coach could see his team improving. It was the third practice when the problems started. Five boys arrived fifteen minutes late to practice. Their teacher, Mr. Hall, had kept them after school for a detention. At the end of the practice, the coach had a discussion with his team about the importance of keeping up with their schoolwork and behaving themselves so that practices and games would not be missed.

The coach then went to speak to Mr. Hall. He reminded Mr. Hall about the staff meeting they had had earlier in the year when they discussed school policy about membership on a sports team. The staff had agreed that there would be a "three strikes and you're out" policy. In other words, if a student who was on a school team misbehaved or did not complete a homework assignment, he or she would be given three chances. The student would be allowed to attend the practice or the game and serve the detention time at a later date (such as at recess the next day) or complete missed homework at home. If the student exceeded three strikes, the student would be off the team.

The policy had been established during volleyball season earlier in the year, mostly because of Mr. Hall's students' attendance problems. He had been keeping his students after school and not allowing them to attend practices, and, sometimes, even games. He had explained his rationale: "School work needs to come first. My students need to learn that. I don't feel right about rewarding them with play when they haven't done their work. My students also need to learn that there are consequences for poor behaviour, and these should be immediate in order for them to be effective."

Other staff members had argued that students benefited from being part of a sports team—they learned valuable skills and attitudes, and it boosted their self-esteem. These things were just as important as academics. After much discussion, Mr. Hall had stated that although he didn't agree with the policy, he would go along with it, as it had the other teachers' support.

The rest of the volleyball season had gone by without incident. Now the basketball coach felt as if he was at square one again with Mr. Hall. Mr. Hall said that he remembered the staff meeting and the sports policy but that today had been an exception. He had been so exasperated by his students' work ethic that he had needed to do something drastic. He then told the coach that, in fact, he was lucky the students had only been kept for fifteen minutes, since they really deserved a much longer detention. The coach told Mr. Hall that he understood, but that he hoped this would not happen again. Mr. Hall said that he hoped so, too.

However, the next week, it did happen again. This time, Mr. Hall had issued a whole-class after-school detention because, when he came into the classroom after lunch, the classroom had been a disaster. Because of rain, the students had stayed inside during lunch break. They had made a mess in the classroom, and they needed to be punished. So none of his students were allowed to attend the practice, which meant that over half the team was missing. There were not enough players to make a practice worthwhile. The coach had had no warning from Mr. Hall that his students would not be showing up.

Again the coach went to speak to Mr. Hall. Again Mr. Hall explained that he had needed to take drastic measures with his class because of their "outrageous" behaviour. This time the coach was not as understanding. He told Mr. Hall that he was not following school policy and that this was not acceptable. Mr. Hall replied that he felt controlling his class was more important than school sports policy. The coach felt like he was getting nowhere. He told Mr. Hall that he was not satisfied with his response and that he wanted to have a meeting with the principal so that she could help them resolve the issue. Mr. Hall agreed, and a meeting was set up for the following morning.

When Mr. Hall arrived ten minutes late to the meeting, he sat down and immediately stated that he was not prepared to change his stance or come to a compromise. He was simply at the meeting to state his position. He repeated his "academics and discipline first" speech. The principal, Janice Wright, told him that he had no choice in the matter. The staff had agreed on the sports policy, and Mr. Hall was obliged to follow it. Mr. Hall argued that it would destroy his ability to manage his classroom and reduce his credibility with his students. Janice refused to argue with him. She simply repeated that Mr. Hall was obliged to follow school policy. She told him that he needed to find other ways to deal with homework and behavioural problems. She offered to help him with this. She then declared the meeting over.

Two days later, the coach stormed into Janice's office. It was 3:00 p.m. "I've had it with Mr. Hall!" he exclaimed, "I have to cancel our first basketball game because we don't have enough players. Mr. Hall has just informed me that he is keeping five of my players after school because they have to rewrite a math test that they failed earlier today. I have already arranged for referees and transportation. I am not happy, and my team will be disappointed."

"Don't cancel your game," replied Janice, as she got up from her desk. She calmly walked down the hall and into Mr. Hall's classroom. "Excuse me," she said, "but would the members of the boys' basketball team please follow me? You have a game to play."

Discussion Questions

* Can teacher autonomy override school policy?
* Is there another way the principal could have handled the situation?
* What are the teachers' rights, and what are their responsibilities in a situation where they disagree with school policy?
* How do you deal with a person who sabotages the decisions of the group?

See appendix, page 135

19

I CAN DO THE JOB

———·——

The staff members at Harmony Elementary had decided at the first staff meeting of the year that they wanted to be a fully inclusive school and that they were willing to "do whatever it takes" for all students to be successful at Harmony Elementary. They stated that they believed that all students can learn and have a right to learn at their own pace. They had agreed that they would employ positive behaviour strategies in their classrooms to teach students expected behaviours. The learning assistance teacher had provided examples of how teachers could modify and adapt their materials for the students in the class who were not at grade level. He had offered to assist teachers to implement these adaptations or modifications. The school also had a school-based team that met every week to discuss any teacher's concerns about particular students. They had access to consultants from the school district who specialized in counselling and testing students who had special needs and specialists in autism spectrum disorder, fetal alcohol spectrum disorder, and speech and language pathology. Principal Janice Wright knew she was lucky to have staff members who were willing to work so hard to meet the needs of every student.

Sally Bright's grade 7 class was the most difficult class in the school. In addition to the regular challenges that came with this age group, Ms. Bright had four students in her class with special needs. One of the students was autistic, and the other three had severe behavioural disorders. Ms. Bright had endured days that she thought would never end, but she had always persevered, and, for the most part, the class was doing well. She knew that this would not be the case if she had not had an excellent student support worker assigned to her class. Rob Ready was well trained and, although he was in the class to support the learning needs of the student with autism, he was also a master at working with the three students with behavioural problems. In February, Rob was diagnosed with cancer. He immediately went on long-term sick leave, and his job was posted. The job posting stated that the applicant should be trained to work with students with autism. Since student support worker jobs are unionized positions, the job went to the person who had the most seniority, and Mary McLean became the newest staff member at Harmony Elementary. She had taken classes about autism but had never worked with autistic students, nor had she worked with students with severe behaviour. Janice explained to her the school's philosophy of including all students and doing whatever it took to be successful with the students. Mary assured her new principal that she would be able to do the job.

Mary was introduced to Ms. Bright and was warmly welcomed into the class by everyone, except the student with autism and the three students with behaviour problems. On her first day, the student with autism bit Mary and screamed that he wanted Mr. Ready "to come back right now." Ms. Bright had to get Janice to cover the class so that she could calm the student down. After the students had left for the day, Ms. Bright and Mary talked about some strategies that Rob had used that worked effectively with the student. Mary said that she would try to implement them. She also let Ms. Bright know that had a bad back and would have difficulty if she had to put the student into a hold. Ms. Bright assured her that this had not been necessary so far this year. Mary asked Ms. Bright what she should be doing with the students who had behavioural problems, because they had been uncooperative with her and had refused her help. Ms. Bright gave Mary the behaviour plan for each student and the notes Rob had left for the person who would replace him. Mary looked discouraged when she left the meeting but said that she was determined to stay in the position.

After two weeks, Mary was still unable to gain instructional control of the student with autism, despite almost daily meetings with Ms. Bright and the school-based team. The student had been sent home three times in the past two weeks, and his parents were not happy with the situation. The students with severe behavioural problems were also falling apart. When Ms. Bright was able to work with them, they would co-operate, but as soon as Mary took over and tried to work with them individually, they would begin swearing and would refuse to do any work. Each of the students had been sent home with suspensions of at least one day for disrupting the class. These were the first suspensions in Ms. Bright's class that year. Finally, after three weeks of trying to work with Mary, a very frustrated Ms. Bright walked into to Janice's office and told Janice that she did not think that Mary had the skills to work with the students in her class. Janice was very busy at that time with another matter and told Ms. Bright, "Just hang in there. I will get around to observing in your class later this week."

The next day, the student with autism had to be placed in the hold because he was out of control and in danger of hurting himself or others. Mary did the hold, but was unable to gain control of the student. He fell, his head hit the bookcase, and he started to bleed. Mary yelled out, "I have hurt my back, someone help me!" Ms. Bright sent a student to get Janice and asked the student to bring back a first-aid kit. As Ms. Bright turned to go to help the autistic student, she noticed Mary sitting, rubbing her back. When Ms. Bright suggested that Mary needed to help her with the student, Mary replied that she was injured and needed to go to the doctor. Ms. Bright looked at Mary and, in frustration, said, "Your job is to keep this student safe and to help him learn. You can't do your job, so you might as well leave. I would give anything to have Rob back."

Janice rushed to the classroom with the learning assistance teacher, and they were able to get the bleeding stopped and to help the student out of the classroom. When school was out for the day, Ms. Bright went to speak with Janice, She told her what she had said to Mary and expressed her frustration with Mary's inability to do the job as well as Rob Ready had. Just then, the phone rang, and Janice answered. It was the head of the union that represented student support workers. He told Janice that Mary had just contacted him and that she would not be returning to work as a result of her back injury. He also told Janice that Mary was filing a grievance because "the principal had failed to provide a safe environment in which to work." He further said that Mary intended to file a harassment complaint against Ms. Bright for her "constant comments about how Rob Ready was so much better at the job" and because Mary had heard through the grapevine that Ms. Bright had told Janice that she was not able to do her job. Janice hung up the phone, looked at Ms. Bright, and wondered what would happen next.

Discussion Questions

* What constitutes a safe working environment in a school? When your job is to support students with special needs, does that change what is considered a safe working environment?
* What constitutes harassment in the workplace? Did Ms. Bright harass Mary?

See appendix, page 136

20

A CRUEL AND UNUSUAL PUNISHMENT

It was February, and the students in Mme Leblanc's French immersion kindergarten class had enough French vocabulary and courage to put words together to form simple French sentences. Mme Leblanc was pleased with her students' progress. She wanted to encourage them to speak as much French as possible while in her class as they were only with her for two and a half hours a day. Then they went home to little or no French until the following school day. She needed to expose them to as much French as possible while they were with her.

Mme Leblanc noticed that during snack time, when she was not directly teaching her students, they always spoke in English to each other. She realized that their communication skills in French were limited, but it bothered her that her students were using any English at this point in the school year. She told her students that she wanted to hear them speaking in French with each other during snack time and that if she heard a student speaking in English, she would ask that student to put his or her snack away until the end of class.

The following day, Mme Leblanc put her plan in action. She reminded her students of the new rule just before snack time. On that first day, quite a few students were asked to put their snack away for speaking English. Some of the students were upset, but Mme Leblanc explained to them why they were asked to put their snack away and that they could eat their snack after school.

As the week progressed, fewer students were being asked to put their snacks away. There were fewer tears, and it appeared that most students had accepted the new rule. Mme Leblanc was pleased to be hearing far less English during snack time. She had found a way to get her students to speak French among themselves.

Vice-Principal Doug Simard received two telephone calls, two visits, and a letter from parents in response to Mme Leblanc's new strategy. All of the parents were unhappy. He had been unaware of Mme LeBlanc's plan until then. The parents felt that taking food from a child was a punishment for speaking English, not an incentive to speak French. They argued that snack time was an important time for kindergarten students and that to take their snacks away was nothing short of cruel. After all, these students were only five years old. Did they really understand the reasons for this consequence? Also, did they know enough French to carry on an unguided conversation with their friends? The parents wanted the practice to stop. Their children were upset, and so were they. When they had approached Mme Leblanc about it, she had been unwilling to change the new rule. She didn't think that the students would starve, and she felt that their French conversation skills were improving as a direct result of her plan.

Doug met with Mme Leblanc. He told her about the complaints he had received. She wanted to know who had complained. She commented that there were some parents in her class who were over-protective. She had already spoken to some of them and asked them to be patient. She was sure that things would settle down once the students caught on. Doug asked Mme Leblanc if she had considered other ways to encourage her students to speak French, such as positive reinforcement and encouragement. Mme Leblanc informed him that she did not believe giving out stickers was effective and that she did not have time for rewards programs. She defended her strategy and told Doug about the positive results she had already witnessed. She heard much less English during snack time. In fact, snack time was quite quiet and pleasant for her now. Mme Leblanc invited Doug to come to her class to observe how well her plan was working.

The following day, Doug spent some time in Mme Leblanc's

class. He observed students at play and then at snack time. He heard students speaking in French to each other, using simple French sentences. Other students ate their snack and were very quiet. A couple of students began to speak in English. They were very excited about a toy that one of them was bringing for show and tell. Mme Leblanc quietly went over to them and asked them to put their snack away. There were tears, but the students complied. The rest of snack time was subdued. Doug got the impression that the students were afraid to speak at all. He had seen enough.

Discussion Questions

* When is it appropriate for an administrator to observe in a classroom based on a parent complaint?
* Based on what the vice-principal observed, what do you think he should do next?

See appendix, page 136

21

PRIVATE LIVES IN THE PUBLIC SCHOOL

As Janice Wright walked into the foyer of the office after observing in a grade 2 physical education class, she was surprised to see the chairperson of the Parent Advisory Council, Mrs. Wilson, and her husband, Alfred, waiting for her. They both appeared distressed and asked if they could speak with her privately. Janice showed them into her office and closed the door. Mrs. Wilson said that she did not know where to begin and that what she was about to tell Janice was to be kept in the strictest of confidence. "Alfred has been charged with a criminal offence. It's sexual assault," Mrs. Wilson said. She added that the charges were untrue and that they were going to fight them. She thought that Janice should know because the family pressing the charges lived in the school community. Although all of the children in that family were in high school, they were well known in the community and had many friends whose children did attend the elementary school. Mrs. Wilson and her husband also wanted to let Janice know what was going on so that she could protect their children from any insults or teasing that could result from the charges. She stated that she was thinking of resigning as the PAC chairperson.

Janice Wright had been patiently listening to them. Her attitude changed from her initial reaction, "Why are you telling me all of this about your private life?" to a realization that what Mr. Wilson had been charged with could really affect the atmosphere in the school. She thanked them for coming in and being so honest with her. She told them that she would be listening carefully for any name-calling or teasing related to this alleged incident. She encouraged Mrs. Wilson to continue with her involvement in the PAC and decided to let the courts decide if anyone was guilty of anything.

Janice did not give the charges against Alfred another thought until a mother with four children in the school came in to see her. She stated that Janice needed to do something about Alfred and his wife's membership in the PAC. She demanded to know whether Janice knew about the charges against Alfred. Janice replied that she was not prepared to discuss the matter. She stated that the courts would decide Alfred's innocence or guilt. Janice politely asked her to leave and let her know that she did not want to hear any more about this from her or from her children. The mother left quietly but was clearly unhappy with Janice.

Alfred and his wife came in again soon after this incident and explained that things did not look good for Alfred and that if he pled guilty and took the plea bargain he had been offered, he would get a lighter sentence than if the case went to trial. Mrs. Wilson maintained that her husband was innocent.

In the end, the case did not go to trial because Alfred pled guilty. He was given a fine, probation, and told to attend a series of counselling sessions for his problems with alcohol. Janice breathed a sigh of relief, as she assumed that the whole time-consuming incident could now be put to rest. There was very little mention of it in the paper and no mention of it at school.

Two weeks later, however, the parents of the girl whom Alfred allegedly assaulted came in to see Janice. After they sat down in her office, they proceeded to tell Janice their side of the story about the assault. They demanded that Janice ban the Wilsons from all school activities. Janice listened to their concerns and then told them that this was a matter for the courts, not the school. As they were leaving, they told Janice that she was not doing her job to protect the children of the school.

The next morning, Janice received a call at home from a very distraught Mrs. Wilson. The girl's family had written a letter to the editor that had been published in the morning paper. It mentioned Alfred's name and stated the facts of the case. It identified where he lived and called him a "sexual predator living in our community." It mentioned that he and his wife were volunteers at the local school.

Later that morning, Janice started getting phone calls. The callers were demanding to know if she had been aware of the charges and, if so, why she had allowed Alfred Wilson's wife to continue as chairperson of the PAC. Janice explained that Alfred's wife was not the convicted person. Students were now aware of the case and had started teasing the Wilson children.

Janice was inundated with calls questioning her credibility.

Discussion Questions

* When is it appropriate for an administrator to get involved with the personal problems of families in the school?
* How can an administrator rebuild his or her credibility in a community?
* What steps could the principal take to protect the Wilson children from comments and teasing?

See appendix, page 137

22

SHOT PUT

———•••———

It was April, and track and field season at Harmony Elementary School was just beginning. It was Vice-Principal Doug Simard's favourite time of year. He had been a track athlete in high school and university and had been heading the track and field program at Harmony for the past three years. This season had started out well. The grade 4 to 7 teachers had agreed to have track and field taught to all of their students for one period in the afternoon, three times a week. The students had been divided into age groups and rotated through stations to learn the basics of each event. Doug was pleased to have all returning teachers helping with track and field this year. They had been to sessions covering common safety precautions and basic techniques, and they had learned coaching techniques for the more advanced students. Doug knew that this was going to be a great year for Harmony Elementary School at the district track meet.

During the second week of the track and field practices, Mr. Edwards, who had been in charge of the shot put station for the past ten years, was rushed into the hospital for surgery. During the same week, Doug Simard had to leave town for a family emergency. Miss Megan Cooper replaced Mr. Edwards in his grade 5 classroom. She was also assigned his shot put duties. The only training she had received was during a quick demonstration of the proper throw by one of the boys in grade 7. She was told not to worry about her lack of expertise because Mr. Edwards had taught the basics to all of the students before he became ill. Despite the fact that Miss Cooper rarely led physical activities, she was confident that she could handle the students during the designated track and field time.

The grade 7 boys were her first group in the rotation. They behaved very well because they were motivated to do well in this event. They lined up and waited patiently for each student to have a turn. The grade 6 boys were next. They were the exact opposite of the grade 7 boys. They refused to stay in line, and they did not listen to anything Miss Cooper said. She was busy talking with a boy who had been rude to her, when she heard a scream of pain. One of the boys had thrown the shot put at another boy because "he wouldn't get out of the way fast enough." The shot put hit the student in the knee. As he lay on the ground, writhing in pain, the other students gathered around, shouting about who was at fault. One student was sent to the office to get the secretary, who was well versed in first aid. Miss Cooper tried to calm the group of grade 6 boys down so that she could begin to sort out the facts. She was so focussed on doing this that she did not notice two of the boys leave the school grounds. The secretary, Mrs. James, arrived and determined that the injured boy's knee should be wrapped in ice and crutches brought down to the field. She left with two students to get the ice packs, wrap, and crutches. While back at the office, she phoned the injured boy's mother and interrupted the principal, Janice Wright, who had been in a meeting, to tell her that there was a problem on the field.

By the time Mrs. James arrived back on the field with Janice, Miss Cooper had managed to quiet the grade 6 boys and get them seated. A jacket had been placed over the injured student so he would not get chilled. Janice asked Miss Cooper to take the boys back to room number five until the track and field practice was over. Mrs. James had just finished wrapping the boy's knee in ice when his mother's car came roaring into the school parking lot. She ran down to the field and hugged her son. Mrs. James attempted to explain to her what she had done for the injury, but the mother cut her off, "I am taking him to the hospital for x-rays.

He had better be all right because he is a star hockey and soccer player. I want to know how this could have happened. If the school is liable in any way for this injury, you will hear from my lawyer." With that, she helped her son up and practically carried him to the car.

Discussion Questions

* What is the first thing Janice, the principal, needs to do? Why? What should she deal with next?
* Explain how an administrator could have predicted and prevented some of the problems faced by Miss Cooper.
* Should the school administrator be concerned about the parent's threat? Why or why not?

See appendix, page 137

23

THE CD

It was April and the grade sevens had started their chant: "This place is so boring. Why can't we go out? We can't do anything here!" Principal Janice Wright knew that, on the one hand, it meant that they were nearly ready for grade 8 and a system where they would have more personal responsibility. On the other hand, there were still two months of school to get through until the final assembly when the grade sevens waved goodbye. The grade 7 teachers at Harmony Elementary school were trying to think of new activities that would keep the students positively engaged during the lunch hour. One enterprising young teacher, Sally Bright, suggested that holding grade 7 dances twice a month during the lunch break would be a good idea. The students would be responsible for selecting the music and getting the gym set up for the lunch hour dances. Janice Wright and Vice-Principal Doug Simard gave Ms. Bright the go-ahead and offered to help with any supervision that might be needed. Mr. Mantel, the other grade 7 teacher, was not in favour of the dances but said that, if needed, he would help supervise.

The first dance was a success. The students did a great job with the music, and they abided by the caveat that there was to be no swearing in the lyrics. The second dance was just as successful. Mr. Mantel did not supervise either dance, but he made it clear that he felt the music was too loud and that the lyrics were questionable. On the day of the third dance, both Janice and Doug had to be away at lunch hour. They asked Mr. Mantel to supervise the dance, and he grudgingly agreed to do so. Although the dance was not to begin until 12:25, Mr. Mantel went down to the gym early to check on the setup. When he entered the gym, he heard swearing coming from the CD player. He went over to the CD player and ejected the CD. Raising his voice, he asked the students gathered whom the CD belonged to. No one replied. He was so incensed with the contents of the song that he broke the CD in half, threw it in the garbage, announced that the dance was cancelled for that day, and stormed off to find Ms. Bright.

The next morning, Cassie House approached Janice. She was one of the students who had been in the gym. She said that the CD that had been broken belonged to her brother, who was in high school. He had purchased it at a hip-hop show. This meant that she could not replace the CD because the group had left town. Cassie said that one of the boys in her class had taken it and put it in the CD player as a joke. She said that she was very sorry for bringing it to school but that she didn't think that teachers had the right to destroy student property.

Janice assured her that she would look into the matter and suggested that since Cassie was in Mr. Mantel's class, she should explain to him what had happened. Cassie said that she would talk to Mr. Mantel right away. Fifteen minutes later, Cassie was in Janice's office in tears. After Janice had calmed Cassie down so that she could speak, Cassie told her that Mr. Mantel had said he had every right to destroy such filthy music and that Cassie should never have brought it to school in the first place. He had refused to reimburse Cassie for the CD.

Janice determined that Mr. Mantel had every right to take the CD away, but he had no right to destroy the personal property of a student. She directed Mr. Mantel to pay Cassie for the full price of the CD.

The following afternoon, shortly after school had been dismissed, Janice received a phone call from Cassie's mother. She was very angry because Mr. Mantel had told her daughter that he would be repaying her in empty cans. He had then handed Cassie a bag full of cans and told her to take them to the bottle depot to get her money back. After Janice talked with Cassie's mother, she called Mr. Mantel to her office.

Discussion Questions

* Can a teacher take personal property from a student and withhold or destroy it?
* What damage has occurred as a result of the teacher's actions (taking the CD and destroying it in front of the students, cancelling the dance, refusing to pay for the CD and then, paying with pop cans)?
* Does this warrant a letter of discipline for the teacher?

See appendix, page 138

24

THE IMPORTANCE OF
FOLLOWING INSTRUCTIONS

It was early May and time to administer the provincial assessments in reading, writing, and numeracy to the grade 4 and 7 students. The teachers were becoming used to these assessments, although many did not feel they were of any use to the classroom teacher. However, they were mandated by the provincial Ministry of Education, and, whether the teachers liked it or not, they would be administered during a two-week period.

Janice Wright had downloaded practice tests for her teachers to use to help prepare the students for writing this type of assessment examination. One teacher, Miss Tyler, expressed her nervousness about the assessments to Janice. Janice recalled that the year before, there had been some problems with the assessments in Miss Tyler's class: some booklets had gone missing, and one student had been instructed by Miss Tyler to do a portion of the assessment she had missed at home so that she wouldn't miss any more class time. Janice had dealt with these problems last year. She hoped that there would be no problems this year. To be on the safe side, Janice suggested that she or the learning assistance teacher administer the tests for Miss Tyler. Miss Tyler refused the offer, saying that she needed to be flexible about fitting the tests into her busy class schedule. She didn't want to be tied down to a particular time on a particular day. Janice told Miss Tyler that she needed to schedule the assessments, and just to "fit them in somewhere." Janice also told Miss Tyler to make sure she read the instructions to teachers very carefully so that she would be fully prepared and not feel nervous when the time came to administer the assessments.

Near the end of the assessment period, Janice received a phone call from the parent of a grade 4 student. This parent was concerned about something her child had told her about the assessments. Her child had asked her about the definition of cheating. Her child then told her that she felt that her teacher, Miss Tyler, was letting some students in her class cheat on the assessments. During the numeracy test, Miss Tyler had taken a group of students to a table in the back of the classroom and explained some of the questions to them. She had then told them to go back to their seats and redo the questions. She had also told them that they could have as much extra time as they needed. The caller's child, one of the students who had received extra help, was not feeling good about what had transpired. The parent did not want to cause a disturbance, but she did want some answers. Janice thanked her for the phone call and said that she would investigate her concern immediately.

Janice decided to drop in on Miss Tyler's class that morning. When she arrived, she noticed that the numeracy test booklets and answer sheets were on the students' desks. She assumed that they were in the middle of writing the test. However, Miss Tyler was at the board at the front of the class, in the middle of an explanation. She welcomed Janice into the class and explained that she and the students were going over all the questions in the test to see what things they knew well and where they needed to do more work. Janice sat and watched for a few minutes. She was concerned—very concerned. As Miss Tyler was explaining, and giving the correct answer, the students had plenty of opportunity to change their answers. Janice interrupted the lesson to ask Miss Tyler if she could speak with her in the hallway. She told Miss Tyler to immediately stop going over the test with her students. She then asked Miss Tyler to meet with her in her office after school that day.

Janice returned to her office and carefully read over the

instructions to teachers and instructions to principals. She wanted to be sure that Miss Tyler understood that the assessments were not to be used for instructional purposes. She found the pertinent instructions and highlighted them. It was clear that Miss Tyler had not been following proper procedure that morning when Janice had visited her class. It remained to be seen whether or not the parent's complaint about cheating was legitimate. After talking it over with her vice-principal and the assistant superintendent, it was evident that an official investigation would have to take place. Janice drafted a letter of investigation and asked the staff union representative to come to her office with Miss Tyler after school.

That afternoon Frank, the president of the teachers' union, showed up in Janice's office. He had received a call from the staff representative, and he had decided that he would support Miss Tyler, in place of the staff representative, because the teachers' union did not agree with the administration of these assessments in the first place. He wanted to closely follow any problems that came out of the administration of the assessments. Janice explained her two concerns to him. First, she had observed Miss Tyler using the numeracy assessment as an instructional tool in her classroom that morning, and her students had had the opportunity to change their answers during that time. Second, she had heard from a concerned parent that students had received help on the math questions from Miss Tyler during the administration of the numeracy assessment, and she was going to investigate this concern.

Frank was surprised by these allegations and was certain that there was a good explanation. Janice explained that Miss Tyler had been nervous about administering the assessments. She had tried to assure her that they would not be a reflection on Miss Tyler's teaching ability. However, it was evident that Miss Tyler had not been convinced of this.

At the afternoon meeting, Janice handed Miss Tyler the letter of investigation and informed her of the concerns outlined in the letter. The next day, Janice began her investigation.

She began by interviewing Kathy, the daughter of the parent who had initially contacted her. Kathy told her that Miss Tyler had taken aside a group of eight students during the numeracy assessment. She had gone over a whole section of the test with these students and then instructed them to return to their seats and to redo the questions. Janice interviewed the other students who had received help. They all told the same story. Some of them indicated that they did not feel comfortable with what had happened. Although they had had little, if any, experience in writing this kind of test, they felt that the "help" that their teacher had given them wasn't right.

Janice then interviewed Miss Tyler, in the presence of Frank. Miss Tyler admitted to having helped a group of students during the numeracy assessment. She explained that the students had been having some trouble with one part of the assessment. She assumed that they had been absent when that particular concept had been taught, so she thought it only fair to teach them the concept. She did not believe, at the time, that she had been doing anything wrong. Janice told her about the phone call from the parent and the feelings about cheating that some of the students had expressed to her. Miss Tyler seemed to be surprised by this. She truly believed that she had acted in the best interests of her students. She only wanted them to do well. However, she now knew differently. Janice then brought up what she had observed when she had visited Miss Tyler's class earlier that week. Miss Tyler explained that she had simply been going over the assessment with her students to explain each question. She said that she had told them that they were just doing this for interest's sake and that they were not to change any of their answers. Janice asked her why the answer sheets were on the students' desks. Miss Tyler replied that she had wanted her students to see where they had gone wrong. Miss Tyler believed that, in this case, she had done nothing wrong. That was the end of the interview.

Janice now had to decide what to do. Miss Tyler had not followed proper procedure in administering the numeracy assessment. The education ministry could not consider the results valid. She phoned the person in charge of the assessments at the ministry and explained what had happened. She asked him what she should do. He told her to send everything in to them. They would most likely not count the numeracy assessments from Miss Tyler's class with the school's data. They would also not report the individual student's results of this assessment to their parents. They would simply mark the students as absent from the numeracy portion. It would be up to Janice to explain this to the parents and the students.

Discussion Questions

* What is the teacher's responsibility regarding the administration of provincial assessment examinations?
* What is the principal's responsibility?
* What should the principal do in the following year in order to avoid further problems?

See appendix, page 138

25

A PERSONAL MATTER

———·———

For the past month or so, things had been less than harmonious in the grade 5 French immersion classroom at Harmony Elementary School. The teacher, Connie Fair, had taken a medical stress leave, and the replacement teacher had required a lot of help from Janice Wright. Once routines had been established, and visits from Janice had become a regular part of the classroom, things began to get better. However, Janice's time was in short supply, and she had been looking forward to Mrs. Fair's return to work.

After Mrs. Fair had been back for a month, Mrs. Braun, another teacher on staff, came into Janice's office. She said that she had just witnessed Mrs. Fair's class out on the field being taught physical education by Mrs. Fair's husband, and Mrs. Fair was nowhere to be seen. Mrs. Braun said that she would be speaking directly to Mrs. Fair about the incident. Mrs. Braun did not want Janice to do anything until she had spoken to her.

The next day, Mrs. Fair came to see Janice and told her that she had made a mistake and that her husband, Simon, had taken the students outside for gym. She said that she had remained in the class for approximately five minutes. Janice explained to her that Simon was not a teacher and could not, under any circumstances, take the class anywhere for any reason. Mrs. Fair said that she was sorry and that it would not happen again.

Janice began to notice that Simon seemed to be at the school on a daily basis, often around lunchtime. It was not until a parent of one of the students phoned her that Janice realized how much time Simon had been spending in Mrs. Fair's classroom. The parent, who was a lawyer, alleged that Simon had been in the classroom for the past week, eating his lunch while the children were working and had, on at least one occasion, told the students to be quiet and listen to their teacher. She also stated that she would be doing a criminal record check on Simon as she had heard that there had been some sort of problem with him in another city. She stated that she did not want Simon anywhere near the classroom. She worried that he might pose a threat to the children. Janice listened to these concerns and explained that Simon was, at times, in the school for his own two children who were enrolled at the school. However, Janice stated that she was unaware that Simon had been in his wife's classroom. Janice assured the parent that she would speak to both Simon and his wife about these incidents.

Janice decided to call Simon to speak to him directly. She told him that she had some concerns about his presence in the school. Janice let him know that she had received complaints from parents in the class. He denied everything and said that he had a right to be in the school his children attended. Janice assured him that he could come into the school if he was invited to volunteer in his son or daughter's classroom, but if he wanted to eat lunch with his wife at school, he was to do so in the school staff room from 12:15 to 1:05 p.m. He yelled that Janice was not prepared to listen to him and then hung up on her.

Discussion Questions

- What are the liability issues in this case?
- How can a busy school administrator supervise all staff effectively?
- Should criminal record checks be done on all volunteers, including the spouses of staff members volunteering in the school? Who is responsible for doing criminal record checks?

- What issues does a teacher face who reports another teacher's behaviour to the principal before talking to the teacher he or she is reporting on?
- Should a principal restrict a parent's comings and goings in the school and on the school grounds?

See appendix, page 139

26

PROTECTING ALL STUDENTS

The grade 4 boys had been particularly challenging this year. Both Principal Janice Wright and Vice-Principal Doug Simard had been dealing with several of these boys on a regular basis. The school counsellor had also been working with a group of five boys twice a week. In small groups and one-on-one, the boys were co-operative and reasonable, but things seemed to fall apart on the playground at lunch hour.

Two boys in particular would "lose it" with each other at least twice a week. Tyrell had a particularly short fuse. He thought nothing of lashing out physically whenever he was provoked. Liam, on the other hand, was more covert in his aggression. He knew how to push Tyrell's buttons, by saying hurtful or provocative things, and he did so on a regular basis. Liam was an outsider and did not generally play with any of the boys. Tyrell and his buddies, who considered Tyrell their leader, always played soccer at lunch.

One day after the lunch hour, there were several grade 4 boys waiting outside the principal's office. Tyrell was so angry that his face was completely red. Janice recognized that he was not yet ready to talk. She took him to sit in the medical room to give him some quiet time. Tyrell's friends were anxious to tell Janice their side of the story. Janice interviewed each of them individually and found out as much as she could.

The boys had been playing soccer when Liam approached them to ask if he could play. His request was denied, especially by Tyrell.

Liam then said something to Tyrell and ran away. Tyrell chased after him, but Liam ducked into the school. Tyrell returned to the game. Later on during the lunch hour, some of Tyrell's friends were getting a drink in the school when they spotted Liam sitting in one of the stairwells, drawing. They approached Liam and asked to see his drawing. Liam showed it to them, and they grabbed it and ran away. Liam chased after them. The boys ran out to the soccer field with the drawing and gave it to Tyrell, who took a look at the drawing of a dragon and then tore it into several pieces. Liam was extremely upset, and he said a few things to Tyrell about Tyrell's mother. These remarks had quite an effect on Tyrell, and in no time he was on top of Liam, punching him. Tyrell completely lost control, and Liam fought back. The other boys had wisely stayed out of it, and a supervisor was soon on the scene. The boys, along with some witnesses, were then brought to the office.

When Janice interviewed Liam, he was still upset but was willing to talk about what had happened. His face was bleeding, and she could see that he was going to have a black eye. The ice pack that the supervisor had given him was helping. When Janice tried to interview Tyrell, he was defensive and aggressive. Although he admitted to having punched Liam in the face, he refused to agree that it was the wrong thing to do. He said he would do it again if he were provoked. He was very angry.

Previously, Janice had warned both Tyrell and Liam that if there was one more incident between them, they would both be suspended. The school had been working hard at conflict resolution, and these boys were just not getting it. She had no choice but to follow through with her suspension threat. She suspended Liam for two days and Tyrell for four days. She was concerned about the safety of the other students because of Tyrell's aggression and lack of remorse. Liam and Tyrell's parents were contacted to come to pick up their sons. Liam's father was reasonable and apologetic. He met with Doug Simard for over an hour, talking about what could be done to help Liam stay out

of trouble. Tyrell's father whisked Tyrell away and was not in-
terested in meeting with the administration. Janice thought
that, like his son, he needed some time to cool down. When their
suspension was over, each boy, accompanied by a parent, was
required to meet with Janice before they would be allowed to
return to school.

When it came time for Tyrell to return to school, his father
phoned and said that he would be unable to meet with Janice that
morning. He asked if the meeting could be rescheduled for that afternoon and if it would be all right if Tyrell returned to school the
following day. Janice said that this would be fine. Tyrell's father
came in at 2:00 p.m. He was much more calm and reasonable. He
explained how upset Tyrell had been about Liam's remark about
Tyrell's mother and that it had pushed him over the edge. Janice
commented that Tyrell seemed to be far too easily pushed over
the edge. She suggested that Tyrell attend some anger management counselling, but Tyrell's father wanted nothing to do with
counselling. He said that he would work with his son himself. He
also said that he had taught his son to defend himself if he ever
felt threatened. Janice again explained the school's policy about
fighting. The meeting ended just a couple of minutes before the
dismissal bell.

The next morning, Janice received a phone call from Liam's
father. He was upset and said that Liam was afraid to go to
school. Apparently, after his meeting with Janice the previous
day, Tyrell's father had gone out to the bus area and found Liam.
He told Liam that if he bothered Tyrell again, he would send
Tyrell's sixteen-year-old brother over to the school to "rip Liam's
face off." Janice phoned Tyrell's father. He admitted to having
threatened Liam. He said that he understood the school's policy
and that he would no longer encourage Tyrell to fight, but his
older son would do what had to be done, and he did not care about
the consequences.

Discussion Questions

* Are there alternatives, other than suspension, that could be more effective in this type of situation?
* Is it appropriate for a parent to try to correct the behaviour of a student on the school grounds who is not his or her own child?

See appendix, page 139

27

SOMEONE HELP ME!

———·•·———

It was five o'clock in the afternoon and Janice Wright was just locking up her office when she looked up to see a student, Amber Jackson, running towards the office. She said some kids had "ganged up" on her. Janice asked if she was hurt, and she said she was not. Since Janice could see that she was upset, she offered to drive her home. She told Amber to write down all of the events that had happened after school and to bring this record in to her first thing the next morning. Amber accepted the ride home and promised to stay in her house, with the doors locked, until her parents got home from work. As Janice continued home, she noticed a group of students from Amber's grade congregated at one of the condominium complexes. She thought about stopping to see if they knew anything about the incident with Amber but decided that it could all wait until the next day.

At 8:10 a.m. the next day, Amber and her father came to see Janice in her office. Amber's dad was distraught about the incident. He threatened to go to the police and to the newspaper if something didn't happen "right now." He further stated that he did not want his daughter attending a school that permitted the "swarming" of students. Janice assured him that she would fully investigate the incident and that she would meet with him after school that day.

Janice spent the entire day interviewing the students who had been involved in the incident. She found out that miscommunication had caused the threatening and taunting. In the end, Amber had been the one responsible for the initial misunderstanding because of something she had said about another girl's boyfriend. Janice spoke to the three girls involved, and they agreed that the whole thing could have been avoided if they had communicated clearly with one another. Amber told Janice that she had not told her parents about her part in the incident but that she would do so that evening. Janice spoke to Mr. and Mrs. Jackson at three o'clock and told them what she had discovered. She also explained to them that their daughter would be talking to them about her part in the incident.

Discussion Questions

* How could Janice have avoided some of the problems if she had dealt with the complaint when it occurred, rather than waiting for the next day?
* What is the principal's responsibility if he or she hears that something is going to happen after school?

See appendix, page 140

28

NOT IN THIS SCHOOL!

In June of the third term, all of the parents of grade 7 students in Harmony Elementary were sent a letter stating that, with parental permission, the students would be allowed to leave the school grounds at lunch. This was a way of preparing the students for next year when they would be allowed off the school grounds at lunch without supervision or parental permission. Parents were to sign the letter and indicate the places that their child had permission to go. Before leaving class for the lunch hour, students were also obliged to write where they were going on the board in the classroom so that their teachers would know where to find them if there was an emergency.

Parents and staff were comfortable with the arrangement, and the students were very happy with their new freedom. The school had been doing this without incident for a number of years. The school was located in a very busy neighbourhood, so the students had many options of where to go for lunch. Most went to one of the fast food restaurants, to the library, or to the skateboard park.

One day during the third week of June, Janice was taking her usual walk around the school grounds near the end of lunch hour. Across the street, she saw a few grade 7 students leaving the local park. When they saw her watching them, they turned and ran back into the park. It was a wooded area, and Janice was only able to see the entrance from the schoolyard. She was puzzled. She did not recall seeing any parental permission letters that indicated that students could be in that park during lunch hour. There were often questionable characters hanging around there. Janice started out for the park to see what her students were up to. By the time she got there, the students were gone. She heard the bell ring, so she went back to the school.

She went to see the grade 7 teacher to find out if these students had permission to be in the park. They did not. Janice knew that she would have to investigate. She interviewed each student individually that she had seen exiting the park. What she learned from them was quite alarming. Many grade 7 students had been at the park. In fact, they had been going there for the past few days. Most claimed they were "just hanging out." But Janice learned that five students had been smoking marijuana in the park on the previous day. She was shocked. None of these students had shown any troubling behaviour at the school before. They were what she considered "good kids." Janice and the vice-principal interviewed all five students. They discovered that one student had brought the marijuana to school and had invited the other four to join her in the park. Then they all went to a secluded area. For all but one of the students (the one who brought the marijuana to school), this was their first experience with marijuana.

Janice consulted the school district policy and sought advice from the superintendent. She had not encountered this type of problem before in her school. The superintendent informed her that normally any student involved in an illegal substance incident was suspended for five days, but that the final decision was up to the administration. Janice and her vice-principal had a lengthy discussion about what consequences they would give the students.

Discussion Questions

* What is the school's liability for the actions of students when they are off the school grounds?
* What consequences do you think would be appropriate?

* How could a code of conduct have helped in this situation?
* Who should be involved in establishing a code of conduct?

See appendix, page 140

29

THE PICTURE

It was the third week in June. It had been a busy year, and Janice Wright was looking forward to the end of the school year and some time off. She was on morning recess duty when a group of grade 6 and 7 girls came up to her. One girl said, "We really have to talk to you about something that has happened to some of the boys. It's really gross, and they don't want you to know about it." Janice let them know that they could tell her whatever it was and that she would deal with it. Three of the girls came in after the noon hour and demanded that Janice "Fire that support worker!" They alleged that a male support worker had drawn a picture of the female anatomy and shown it to three grade 7 boys. Using the drawing, he had shown them where they could touch their girlfriends to "make them feel really good." Janice listened to the girls and took some notes. When they were finished, she sent them back to their class. She considered what they had told her and decided since it was 2:30 on a Friday afternoon and one of the boys involved was absent, she would deal with it on Monday.

Monday morning arrived and so did a phone call from the mother of one of the boys. As Janice was assuring her that she would be looking into the matter, the mother of one of the other boys was in the school office asking the secretary if she could speak to Janice. The mother came into the principal's office and told Janice that her son had told her what had happened but that he did not want his mother to go to see her. Evidently, the support worker had told the boys that he could get in trouble and maybe even lose his job if they told anyone that he had shown them the picture. Janice told her that she would be speaking to the boys individually and that she would get back to her.

Janice spoke to the each of the boys individually. Their stories were all the same. The support worker had approached them in the computer lab one day just as they were leaving for recess. He asked them if they wanted to see something. They said they did. He closed the door and proceeded to produce the drawing and show them, with his fingers on the paper, what he was talking about. They were all too embarrassed to speak to Janice about the incident. The support worker had thrown the picture away.

Discussion Questions

* Should the principal have acted on the information she received on Friday afternoon rather than waiting until Monday morning? What are the advantages and disadvantages of her decision to wait?
* Was the support worker properly supervised? What constitutes the proper supervision of personnel?

See appendix, page 141

30

WHAT TO DO?

Janice stared in disbelief at Sally Bright, a grade 7 teacher at Harmony Elementary. Ms. Bright had just confided in her about a dilemma she was facing. She wanted Janice's advice.

Ms. Bright had been a high school teacher for the five years prior to coming to Harmony Elementary School. She had been a popular teacher at the high school because she had related well to the problems faced by her adolescent students. Ms. Bright was moved to the elementary school because of declining enrolment at the secondary school. There had been an outcry from her students when she left. Janice knew that many of her former students still called and emailed her to discuss what was happening in their lives. It was one such phone call that had brought Ms. Bright into Janice's office.

Yvonne had been in grade 8 when Ms. Bright had first taught her. They had kept in touch since Ms. Bright moved to Harmony Elementary. Yvonne was just finishing her grade 10 year in school. She had phoned Ms. Bright early that morning and told her that she had just had sex for the first time on the previous night. Her boyfriend had worn a condom, but she said it had come off. She was distraught and very concerned that she could be pregnant. She wanted Ms. Bright to get her the morning-after pill. Ms. Bright told Janice that she had talked to Yvonne about safe sex and the responsibilities that go along with being sexually active. Ms. Bright wanted to know, though she was not currently teaching the girl, whether she should get the pills for Yvonne.

Ms. Bright viewed it as helping a friend and felt that she would have wanted someone to do the same for her if she were at that age and in the same situation. Janice felt that Ms. Bright could not abdicate her role as a teacher in this instance. She told Ms. Bright that she should suggest to Yvonne that they both sit down and speak to Yvonne's parents about what had happened. Failing that, Janice suggested that she should encourage Yvonne to go and see her family physician. Ms. Bright listened to Janice's suggestions and then announced that she knew what she had to do.

Discussion Questions

* What is the relationship between a former teacher and students who are still under the age of majority when dealing with issues that require a moral judgement to be made?

See appendix, page 142

31

SHARED DECISION MAKING

It was nearing the end of the school year and the time when administrators turned their thoughts towards staffing. It was Janice's second year as a principal in the district. Janice was feeling confident and happy with what was happening at her school. She had an enthusiastic and co-operative staff that had been very supportive of the way in which Janice was running the school and of the changes that Janice had initiated. The teachers felt that their opinions were not only valued but also sought after by the administration. Janice made a consistent effort to involve her staff in decision-making processes whenever possible. For example, a budget committee had been established when staff had indicated a desire to have input into how money was spent, and a discipline committee had been created to review behaviour referrals on a monthly basis.

Now it was time to look at staffing for the next school year. There would be two vacancies at Harmony Elementary. Janice asked the teachers if they would like to be part of a staffing committee to help decide on the new teachers. Two teachers volunteered. Also on the committee were two parents who had been appointed by the Parental Advisory Council. All the members of the staffing committee were told that they would be involved in reading over résumés, selecting candidates for the short list, deciding on questions that should be asked at the interview, interviewing candidates, and giving their input to the principal and vice-principal about whom to select for the two positions. It was made clear to all members of the staffing committee that the final decision would be the principal's. All members of the committee were in agreement with the process and their responsibilities.

The committee selected seven applicants to interview. All applicants selected were teachers from the district who were either looking for a change or whose temporary position in the district was ending. All applicants were informed that they would be interviewed by the staffing committee, and they all agreed to the process.

The interviews took place at the school one evening. Before the interviews started, Janice explained to her committee that what was to be discussed during and after the interviews was strictly confidential. The interviews went smoothly, and Janice was pleased with how well the members of the committee had worked together. After each interview, they discussed the applicant's strengths and suitability for the position. At the end of the meeting, each member was given the opportunity to state their first choice for each of the jobs. As it turned out, everyone on the committee had made the same choice. Janice thanked them for their input and told them that she would make the final decision the following day and let them know. All committee members told Janice that they felt good about the process. Both of the parents and both of the teachers stated that they felt that they were valued and that their input was important. Janice was happy to get their input. Staffing was a big responsibility, and she wanted to get it right.

That night, Janice received a phone call at home. It was almost 11:00 p.m. She wondered who would call at that time of night. She thought that it must really be an emergency. The call was from Dave, a member of the teachers' union executive and a parent at Janice's school. He said that he had heard about her staffing committee and that he didn't think it was a very good idea. He was quite upset about the interview process and told her that it was unethical to involve teachers. He said that he was sure that the applicants felt intimidated by the process and that Janice had been out of line in establishing this committee.

Now it was Janice's turn to get upset. She restrained herself, however, and told him that she would be happy to meet with him and the union president on the following day to discuss his concerns. She told Dave that she was not pleased at being phoned at home at such a late hour when it was not an emergency. Dave replied that he felt that it was an emergency. Janice told him that his emergency could wait until tomorrow.

By the time she hung up the phone, Janice was fuming. What right did Dave have to contact her at home and criticize a process that she had put in place in her school? She had discussed the idea of a staffing committee with Frank, the president of the teachers' union, who had been very supportive. They had worked out the process together. How could Dave say that he was representing the teachers' union?

The following morning, Janice phoned Frank as soon as she got to work. However, she learned that Frank was out of the province at a conference and was not expected back until the following week. It was Thursday. Janice decided that she was going to have to meet with Dave on her own. Just then, Sally Bright, one of the teachers on the staffing committee, came into Janice's office. It seemed that she too had received a late-night phone call from Dave, and she had been "blasted" by him for participating in the staffing committee. She was upset. She said that she had felt so positive about the whole process until Dave's phone call. Now she felt "sick" about it.

Janice phoned Dave and set up a meeting with him for later that morning. She then phoned the superintendent and reconfirmed with him that it was indeed within her rights to establish a staffing committee. He assured her that the process she had followed was acceptable in the district but that she was the only principal in the district who had followed this route. The other principals who had been in the district for quite some time had followed more traditional processes when selecting new staff. The superintendent said that he applauded Janice for attempting to be a collaborative decision-maker and gave her his support.

After recess that same morning, Sally Bright arrived in Janice's office in tears. She said that some staff members had been chastising her for participating on the staffing committee. They told her that she should have never agreed to participate. It seemed that Dave had been very busy on the phone with several members of Janice's staff. He seemed to be trying to ruin what should have been a very positive process. Now Janice was angry. She prepared herself for her meeting with Dave.

Discussion Questions

* What are the advantages and disadvantages of involving partner groups in selecting new teachers for a school?
* What else could the superintendent have done to support Janice?
* How should the principal respond to Dave?

See appendix, page 142

32

TO SKIP A GRADE?

On the last day of school, Janice Wright sat in her office and breathed a sigh of relief. The year had been a success. She then looked up to see Mrs. Brown, the parent of a grade 4 student, enter her office. She appeared to have something on her mind. She said, "Thank goodness this year is over. What is our plan for my daughter, Lisa, for next year? I want her to be accelerated and go into grade 6, not grade 5." Janice was caught completely off guard by this comment. The last time she had heard from Mrs. Brown had been in the fall when she had come in to discuss her daughter's lack of interest in completing her homework. Janice had had no indication from Lisa's teacher that Lisa should be considered for acceleration. Janice suggested that Mrs. Brown come in the following day to discuss the matter further. Mrs. Brown agreed to come in at 9:30 a.m. As she was leaving, she said, "I know that you will put her in grade 6 because that is what should happen." Janice left her office and went to see Lisa's teacher to tell her about the conversation that had just taken place. Mrs. Chen, Lisa's teacher, was not in favour of her skipping a grade, and she grudgingly agreed to come to the meeting on the following day.

At the meeting the next morning, Mrs. Brown made it clear that the planned organization of the school for September was unacceptable. It meant that her daughter would have the same teacher two years in a row, and she was adamant that her daughter should skip a grade. After listening to Mrs. Brown's complaints about the shortcomings of the school and her daughter's need for a challenge, Janice explained, that she could do one of two things, but, she patiently explained that putting Lisa into grade 6 was not one of the options. Janice told Mrs. Brown that she could wait until September to see if the class organization changed due to declining or increasing enrolment and, if it did not change, and Lisa was with the same teacher for a second year, the school would ensure that she received some enriched programming. Or Mrs. Brown could enrol her daughter in the larger elementary school six kilometres down the road. Mrs. Brown repeated her initial position, "My daughter is bright, so she belongs in a grade 6 classroom with a new teacher." No one at the meeting disputed Mrs. Brown's assertion that her daughter was bright; however, Mrs. Chen reminded her that her daughter's work habits were quite poor. She said that after teaching her for the last year, and based on her twenty years' teaching experience prior to that, she could not support a plan to accelerate her. At this point, Mrs. Brown became very agitated. She rose from her chair, looked Janice directly in the eye and exclaimed, "You are not giving me any options!" Janice calmly explained that she had given her two options. These options, however, did not happen to be options that Mrs. Brown wanted to hear about. Janice encouraged her to go home and to talk to her daughter about the situation and to get her opinion. Mrs. Brown did not like that suggestion, either. She rose and stated, "Well, since I have no options here, I know what I have to do." She turned on her heel and walked out.

Discussion Questions

- What factors should be considered when a child is being considered for acceleration?
- What factors should be considered when a parent makes a student placement request of an administrator?
- What does an administrator risk and/or gain when he or she chooses to disagree with a vocal parent?

* Do parents know the criteria for acceleration?
* Could the principal have dealt with the parent differently?

See appendix, page 143

PROBLEM
of the DAY

1. A parent is unhappy that her child has been placed in a particular grade 5 class because the other grade 5 teacher does more hiking and outdoor activities. She wants the principal to guarantee that her child will go on the same hikes and do the same outdoor activities if she "agrees" to keep her child in the original class.

2. A parent thinks that the school is not addressing a bullying problem in which she feels her son is the victim. She comes onto the playground and admonishes a child for an incident that allegedly happened the previous day.

3. A parent volunteer is making photocopies for her child's teacher. A teacher who is on his preparatory time impolitely tells the parent to stop photocopying because he needs to use the machine and that teachers on prep. have priority over parents.

4. The school's entrance is on a very busy street, and so the city decides to change the street in front of the school into a no-stopping zone because of safety concerns. The school informs the parents in a newsletter prior to the change. After the zoning changes, a parent writes a letter to the school that states that he is extremely unhappy that he received a ticket when he parked in front of the school for "just a minute" while he went into the school to pick up his children. He claims that the school did not do a good enough job of informing parents of the change.

5. At a PAC meeting, the subject of student awards and recognition is brought up. The parents want more students to be recognized more often for achievement, and not just at the awards assembly at the end of the year. In consultation with teachers it is decided that after each report card, an honour roll will be published in the newsletter and also posted in the school. Grade 4 to 7 students receiving all As and Bs, or all "Goods" in the effort column, will be on the honour roll. They will also receive a

certificate from the principal. After the first honour roll is published in the newsletter, a parent writes a letter to the principal and copies it to the superintendent. The parent is extremely unhappy that the school is doing this. The parent does not agree with the whole concept of the honour roll but takes issue especially with the publication of the list in the newsletter. This parent had not attended the PAC meeting where this had been discussed and decided upon.

6. A teacher reports to the principal that he witnessed another teacher take papers from the principal's letterbox and then photocopy them. These papers were some report cards that had been put there for the principal to sign. The report cards did not belong to the teacher who removed them and photocopied them.

7. A substitute teacher who had been covering a grade seven class for the day left the school as soon as the bell rang at the end of the day. The following day, both the custodian and the teacher who had been absent complain to the principal about the mess that the class has been left in.

8. A teacher's classroom is consistently in a state of disorder. The principal has many chats with the teacher and offers many suggestions on how to keep things more orderly and organized. However, no improvement is made. Then, the Health and Safety Committee cites the classroom as a danger during a school health and safety inspection. Still, the teacher does not organize her classroom. The principal then writes a letter to the teacher and warns the teacher that further action might be necessary if the classroom is not cleaned up and safety concerns are not dealt with. In response, the teacher charges the principal with harassment.

9. The parents of a grade 6 student tell the principal that their daughter is not advancing as quickly as they would like. They also state that she is not receiving satisfactory feedback and reinforcement for her efforts in school from her two teachers. The parents insist on setting up a weekly thirty-minute meeting with both teachers in order to obtain about a report on their child's progress.

10. The band teacher tells one of his students that she needs to choose between band and basketball because the student misses one of the three weekly band practices due to an after-school basketball game. Basketball season is three months long, while band lasts the whole year. The student also takes flute classes outside of the school. The student's mother is unhappy because she wants her daughter to be part of the basketball team and feels that her daughter will be able to keep up with the band even if she plays basketball. The band teacher disagrees.

11. A parent blames the teacher for every problem her son has at school. It is the teacher's fault when the student is disruptive, rude, or non-compliant. She has told the principal that she "can't stand" the teacher. What should the principal do to improve the situation for the parent, the student, and the teacher?

12. A part-time teacher is struggling with curriculum implementation and with classroom management. The principal has received complaints from parents as well as from the students in the class. The principal has talked to the teacher and even demonstrated lessons in the class. The teacher maintains that the problem is not his, as he does not have problems in the other school where he teaches part-time. The principal knows that this is not true, but rather that the principal of the other school does not have time to deal with the teacher's performance. The teacher blames the students and the principal for the problems. He has complained to the union that "the building administrator is not being supportive of me in my class." How can the principal satisfy the parents and the union and help the teacher improve his practice?

13. A support worker phones the school to say that she will not be in due to a problem with her back. However, a parent reports to the principal that on that same day, the support worker is at the local track helping to set up for a track meet.

14. A teacher always gets "sick" for at least two days around report card writing time. Other teachers have noticed and mentioned this to the principal.

15. While the school secretary is away in the hospital for tests for three days, the principal develops some concerns about the replacement secretary's ability to do the job. When the school secretary returns to work, she tells the principal, "Things are in a real mess," and she spends two days straightening things out. In the end, fifty dollars remain unaccounted for.

16. A mother comes to the school at least five times to see the school administration to complain that her son is being bullied. The administration is aware that her son creates many problems for himself by being a provocative victim. The administrators are working with her, the other students, and her son. One day after school, a boy hits her son in the head. She immediately calls to demand the name and phone number of the other student, because she wants to go to the RCMP and report the incident. She says, "I have had enough of this. I want the police to solve it."

17. Two brothers who attend the school are regularly late. One morning, the older brother arrives without his younger brother. He says that his mother did not come home the night before and that he could not wake his little brother. What should be done with this information?

18. A student belonging to a well-known family in the community comes to the office asking for an ice pack. When asked why she needs it, she says that her jaw hurts because that morning, her dad hit her in the face with his fist. She goes on to tell how after that, he dragged her down the stairs and shoved her in the car. She does not appear to have any bruises or red marks, but she is insistent that these things happened. The principal knows the parents, and in the past, the student had told untrue stories.

19. A thirteen-year-old boy in a special education class storms out of the school and is later picked up by a worker from his foster home. In the vehicle he says, "I want to shoot that teacher's face off with my gun." This is reported to the principal. The student has a history of making threats.

20. The principal is new in a school that is staffed with teachers who have had difficulty in other schools. The previous principal was a "good guy" who was willing to take any teacher onto his staff. The new principal discovers that the staff have not been following several district policies. How does the new principal change past practice?

21. The principal receives a phone call at home on a Sunday morning. The caller identifies herself and tells the principal that she saw a teacher on staff on Saturday night out in the bar drinking with a student from the local high school.

22. The new principal at an elementary school notices that many teachers have been placing students on modified programs if they are not working at grade level in a particular subject. The staff explain that they do this so that the students do not have to fail the subject. The principal is not comfortable with this practice because it does not follow the reporting guidelines, and he wants his teachers to try other strategies before placing students on modified programs. What should the principal consider in making a change to this practice? What circumstances should the principal suggest be in place before students are placed on modified programs?

23. A student in grade 7 class is caught with alcohol. The vice-principal talks to him and realizes that he has been drinking. The student is brought into the vice-principal's office and is told that he will be suspended. When the student's father arrives at the school at 4:30 to pick him up, it is obvious that he has also been drinking. What should the vice-principal do?

24. Just before Christmas, the mother of twin boys in grade 2 French immersion comes to see the principal. She says that she wants to transfer both boys to an English grade 1 class in another school because one of the boys is struggling. She explains that she wants to do this so that they can get a good base, and she does not want them separated into different grades because they are twins. The twins were born in November, so they are young compared to the rest of their class. They have been receiving a lot of support at school through learning assistance. How should the principal respond to the parent?

25. The principal has been asked by the staff to defend his discipline policies. The staff feels that the principal is weak and unable to establish a bottom line with students. They want students to be suspended from school after three referrals to the office. The principal is trying to establish a more positive school culture that will enable students to learn how to behave appropriately while at school. The principal schedules a meeting with his staff to talk about this. He also askes a presenter who has been very effective in helping schools establish a positive culture to attend the meeting. The morning of the presentation, the president of the teachers' union arrives at the school and informs the principal that a staff member has asked her to attend the presentation because she does not feel supported by the principal. What should the principal do?

APPENDIX

POSSIBLE ENDINGS *and* RESOLUTIONS

1 • I Am Not Racist!

Janice arranged to see Ms. Gillespie that afternoon. Ms. Gillespie admitted to making the remarks about the Aboriginal students to Joe. She explained that she wanted the best for all students but that based on her experience while growing up, students needed to have high expectations set for them. The colour of their skin was no excuse. Janice asked her if she thought that her comments had damaged her credibility in the classroom with her students and with Joe. She admitted that they probably had. She agreed to be reassigned to another position in the school district.

2 • Split Decisions

The next morning Mr. Evans appeared at Janice's office door. Janice invited him to sit down. "I accept the assignment you have given me," Mr. Evans said in a calm voice, "and I'm sorry for causing a scene. I'll do my best to make it work."

Janice thanked Mr. Evans and told him that she knew he would do an excellent job. Janice also told him that she would help him in any way she could. At the end of that school year, Mr. Evans told Janice that it had been one of the best years of his teaching career. He also volunteered to teach the combined class the following year, should there be one. He even said that he hoped there would be one. It was Janice's turn to smile.

4 • Hormones or Harassment?

Janice then phoned Amy's and Alison's parents to let them know what she had done about the problem. She explained that she felt that most of what had been happening was linked to incidents that had occurred over the summer and, more recently, on weekends. She also told them that she had learned that many of the things that Nicole had allegedly said had been relayed to Amy and Alison by other girls in grade 7. In fact, neither of the girls had actually heard Nicole say any of these inappropriate things.

Janice told their parents that she was prepared to work with the girls to help sort out the problems at school.

Janice explained to their parents that she could not control what happened outside of school and that it was not realistic of them to expect her to deal with an incident that had happened on the weekend or over the summer holidays. Their requests that Janice expel Nicole would not be considered. Janice made it clear that this decision was based on her information, not theirs. She told them that her role was to act as an advocate for all students and she felt that in this case she had done that. She also told them that the counsellor was prepared to work with the three girls to help them sort things out and to provide them with some conflict-resolution strategies.

Alison's parents were in support of the counsellor working with the girls as long as all three girls were involved. Amy's parents would only agree to the counselling if Amy's mother could be present at the sessions. Janice was finally able to get in touch with Nicole's mother. She did not want Nicole to participate in any kind of counselling.

Janice felt frustrated. She knew that these girls needed a counsellor to help them sort through their conflict. She wondered what more she could have done and hoped that the problem would sort itself out without further incident.

5 • Emergency Procedures

Later that afternoon, Janice learned that Mr. Mantel had first heard about the fire on his walkie-talkie about ten minutes before the lunch bell. There had been a parent helping in his classroom at that time. He had asked the parent to supervise his class for the last ten minutes so that he could go and fight the fire. The parent had agreed to do this.

The following day, Janice met with Mr. Mantel and Frank, the president of the teachers' union. Janice explained to Mr. Mantel why she was not happy with his actions. Janice again explained that his primary responsibility was assuring his students' safety. She told him that it was inappropriate for him to leave a parent in charge of his class and that it was inappropriate to expect the school to cover for him while he was off fighting fires. She then handed him a letter of direction that directed him to stay at the school in the event of a fire during his teaching time. The letter also stated that any further incidents of this nature would result in disciplinary action.

The following year, Mr. Mantel resigned from his teaching duties. He moved away to become a paid fire fighter.

6 • The Emailed Complaint

Janice wrote a letter to Mr. Tate outlining the accusations that had been brought against him. In the letter, she asked Mr. Tate to meet with her at his earliest convenience so that she could outline the investigative process. Mr. Tate and the staff union representative came to Janice's office that afternoon. Janice conducted the investigation the following day. She concentrated on the allegations of yelling, grabbing the child's face, and throwing objects. She did not let Mr. Tate know about the original email from Mrs. Black that had been sent to both her and the superintendent.

Janice asked every child in Mr. Tate's class seven questions. She interviewed parent helpers as well as the class's student support worker. By the end of the day, she felt she had completed the investigation. She called Mr. Tate and the staff representative into her office and told them of her preliminary findings. She stated that there was no evidence to support the allegation that he had grabbed a child's face. However, there was evidence that he had, on occasion, thrown things. There was overwhelming evidence that he had used yelling as a means of classroom control. Mr. Tate replied that he had not thrown anything—the pencil had been in his hand and had come loose when he had waved his hand around to make a point. He did not feel that he yelled any more than any other teacher in the school. He also told Janice that he felt he had a very difficult class that year.

Janice used her notes from the interviews and from her meeting with Mr. Tate to write her report. Her final statement was that there was no evidence to support the allegations, except for the allegation of yelling. She sent her report to the superintendent's office and to the personnel department for filing in Mr. Tate's file.

7 • The Reality of ADD

After the meeting, Janice went to see Mr. Edwards. He was alone in his classroom. She let him know that his comments had been inappropriate and that he needed to find a way to meet Kyle's learning needs in the classroom. She also told him that his comment about not believing in ADD had been out of line and that ADD was real and something that he needed to come to terms with and learn to deal with effectively. She suggested that he learn about ADD and research it thoroughly.

The next morning, Kyle's parents came to see Janice. They said that they had decided to move Kyle to another school for the remainder of the year. They saw no point in continuing with Mr. Edwards because they felt that the situation could not be remedied. Kyle could not continue to feel the way he felt in Mr. Edwards' class. Janice had no suggestions to make. If Kyle had been her child, she probably would have done the same thing.

8 • When a Parent Misbehaves

That night, Janice phoned Justin's parents and told them that the saxophone had been found. They were grateful and assured Janice that Justin would take better care of his things. Janice then phoned Carolyn to thank her again and to let her know what had happened. Janice considered herself very fortunate to have such vigilant staff. The detective later phoned Janice at home to let her know that Dawn had agreed to the terms of the restraining order and had said that she would not come onto the school grounds. She would drop Jade off and pick her up outside the school gate. The detective informed Janice that if Dawn violated this order and came onto the school grounds, any staff member could order her to leave. If she refused, or caused any problems, they were to phone the police immediately.

The next morning, Janice called a short staff meeting and explained the situation. Many staff already knew who Dawn was since she had already made quite an impression on many people in the school. Dawn obeyed the order and stayed off the school grounds. Sadly, a few months later, she was involved in a drug bust. Soon after, she left town with Jade. Janice felt powerless. It wasn't fair that a child as young as Jade should have to go through so much because of poor parenting. She wished that she could have done more for Jade.

9 • Report Card Dilemmas

Ivy's mother did not follow through on her threat. As the year progressed, there was no improvement in Ivy's work or in her work habits. She continued to receive Cs and C+s in most of her subjects. The family did move the following year, and Ivy was enrolled in a public school.

10 • Hands Off!

The next morning, Janice phoned the superintendent to give him a heads-up about his potential visitors. He was supportive of her position, and he asked her why she had let the discussion go on for over thirty minutes. He gave her some good advice: "If you fear that a meeting will not go well and you are by yourself, it is best to postpone it until you have the support you need." Janice took pride in her open-door policy, but she now realized that she had to be a little more cautious.

The parents never did go to the superintendent, and Janice did not hear from them again for the remainder of the school year.

11 • Parent Helpers?

Janice shared the concerns raised in the letter with the staff at their next meeting. They decided to form a committee of staff members and parents to develop a parent volunteer handbook. Janice asked Mrs. Fielding to join the committee, but she declined. One week later, she moved her daughter to another school.

12 • The Victim

Doug had just finished reading the letter when he looked up to see Mr. Elleck asking the school secretary if he could speak to the vice-principal. Doug had dealt with Mr. Elleck before and knew he would have to let him vent before he would listen to anything. Doug invited him in. When Mr. Elleck was done with his speech, Doug once again explained the school's philosophy on bullying. He reviewed the numerous initiatives that the school had undertaken to curb the problem. He showed Mr. Elleck the data he had collected over the past two years indicating a drop in bullying incidents. He acknowledged that Mr. Elleck had made some good points in his letter and said that that he would speak to the staff about improving student supervision. However, Mr. Elleck remained firm in his conviction that his children had a right to fight back and that the school needed to do more to create a safe environment for the students.

13 • Appropriate School Clothing

Doug listened to their concerns. He knew that the first three concerns were valid. He was not aware of the candy incident, but he knew Ms. Hatter had told him about her rather strict nutritional policy. He was starting to wonder if he should have taken a more active role in supervising the classroom. Karl's parents informed Doug that they would be writing a letter to the school board outlining their concerns and asking that the teacher be reprimanded. Doug acknowledged that they had a right to do that, but he felt that speaking to the teacher would be a more positive approach. He excused himself from the meeting to arrange for Ms. Hatter's class to be covered so that she could speak to Karl's parents. He then went to get Ms. Hatter from her classroom. As they walked back to Doug's office, he told her that she owed Karl's parents an apology. She agreed. During the meeting, all parties were allowed to have their say, and Ms. Hatter apologized for her actions. Karl's parents accepted the apology and asked that Karl not be placed in her classroom for the following year. Doug was able to meet that request.

15 • Duty of Care

Doug met with the staff members, the community support worker, and the social worker to develop strategies to include in Darren's individualized education plan. They focussed on what Darren could be taught to do when he was not happy at school, instead of running away. They also developed a new safety plan to follow if Darren did run away. All members of the meeting signed off on the new individualized education plan.

18 • A Matter of Policy

Janice included the school policy about membership on a sports team on the agenda for the next staff meeting. At the meeting, they discussed the policy at length. Mr. Hall argued against it forcefully, but the other teachers supported it. In the end, Mr. Hall said that he was going to speak to the president of the teachers' union because he felt that the policy was infringing on his autonomy as a teacher. Mr. Hall left before the meeting was over.

The next day, Frank, the union president, met with the teachers, including Mr. Hall, in the staff room. Janice was not invited. Shouting could be heard coming from the staff room. The meeting lasted over an hour. After it had finished, Frank met with Janice and told her that there would be no further problems with Mr. Hall and the school policy regarding membership on a sports team. There were not; however, the relationship between Mr. Hall and the other teachers remained strained for the rest of the year. At the end of the school year, Mr. Hall requested a transfer to another school.

19 • I Can Do the Job

Janice and Frank, the president of the teachers' union, met with the human resources director to determine if there were grounds for the grievance to proceed. They came to the conclusion that Janice had provided a safe working environment but needed to have an orientation session at her school for all new support workers. The grievance was not carried forward. Mary did not file a harassment complaint. She was reassigned to a different job in the school district and agreed to attend additional training before she took another job with a student with autism. Janice and Ms. Bright reviewed the proper protocol to follow when there were concerns about the job performance of another staff member.

20 • A Cruel and Unusual Punishment

Doug met with Mme Leblanc after her class and told her that he could not let this practice continue. He told her that withholding food in order to encourage students to speak French and punishing them for speaking in their mother tongue was cruel and not inappropriate for such young children. He offered to help her find an acceptable plan. He also encouraged her to go and to observe other teachers to find out how they encouraged their students to speak in French. Mme Leblanc wanted nothing to do with this. She told Doug that she was extremely annoyed that her administrator had interfered with her professional autonomy and had told her to change her practice. She accused him of caving in to parental pressure. She demanded another meeting, with her union representative present.

At the meeting with the union representative, it was clear to Doug that the union representative was uncomfortable. She had a difficult time supporting Mme Leblanc. It was also clear that Mme Leblanc was still angry about his decision and was unwilling to change her practice. Doug finally said, "Whether you agree with me or not, the practice of asking your students to put away their snack when they speak English will stop. You must obey this directive." Although Doug was not used to having to issue directives to his staff, he felt that he had no alternative. The practice stopped, but the relationship between Doug and Mme Leblanc remained strained for the rest of the year.

21 • Private Lives in the Public School

Janice met with Mrs. Wilson and discussed the concerns that were being raised in the community. Mrs. Wilson resigned from the PAC and told Janice that the family would be moving in one week and until that time she intended to keep her children at home.

22 • Shot Put

Janice asked Miss Cooper to write an accident report about what had happened on the field and to bring it to her before leaving for home that day. She also asked Mrs. James to log into the medical procedures journal what type of care and treatment had been administered. Janice began interviewing witnesses and soon discovered that the student who had caused the accident was no longer at school. The other students said he had left with a friend right after the accident happened. Janice phoned the homes of both boys and spoke with their parents. They agreed to come in with their sons the next morning.

When Miss Cooper brought the report into Janice's office, Janice asked her if she realized that two boys had left the school grounds during the incident. She did not reply. After Janice went over the report, she asked Miss Cooper if there was anything that she could have done differently to prevent the accident from happening. Miss Cooper stated that she had not done anything wrong and that if the students at Harmony Elementary School were better behaved, this type of thing would not happen. She refused to take any responsibility for the incident and told Janice she never wanted to be a substitute teacher at Harmony again.

Janice wrote a letter to the human resources director advising him of what had happened and of Miss Cooper's attitude. The boy who had thrown the shot put was suspended for three days and was asked to enrol in anger management classes. He and his parents agreed to meet with the injured boy to apologize to him. The other boy who had left the school grounds without permission was given a three-day in-school suspension. The boy who was injured had to use crutches for one week while his bruised knee healed. His mother did not sue the school. Janice and two teachers put together a track and field guide for substitute teachers and revised the supervision schedule to allow for increased supervision on the field when there was a substitute teacher.

23 • The CD

Mr. Mantel told Janice that he had only been joking when he gave the cans to Cassie. He said that he realized he had used poor judgement. Janice reminded him that she had directed him to pay Cassie for the ruined CD. She then told him that she was once again directing him to pay Cassie, and this time he was to include a letter of apology with the payment. Mr. Mantel complied.

24 • The Importance of Following Instructions

After consulting with the assistant superintendent, Janice drafted a letter of direction to Miss Tyler, a copy of which would be placed in her personnel file. In it, she directed Miss Tyler not to stray from the exact instructions in the teachers' booklet. She also told her that if she had any questions, she should request clarification. Any further problems with the administration of the provincial assessments could result in disciplinary action. Miss Tyler accepted the letter and apologized for her actions. She assured Janice that she would follow the instructions to the letter.

Janice then had the task of informing the students and the parents that the numeracy assessment results would not going to be reported because of an error in the administration of the tests. She needed to let the students know that they had done nothing wrong but that their teacher had made a mistake. It promised to be a very delicate discussion—one that Frank, the union president, did not want to miss. Janice asked herself why she had not insisted in the first place that she or the learning assistance teacher administer the assessments for Miss Tyler. She should have relied on her intuition. Next year things were going to be different!

25 • A Personal Matter

Janice told Mrs. Fair about the conversation she had had with her husband. Mrs. Fair was upset by what he had done, apologized for his behaviour, and said that she would talk to him. Janice then wrote a letter to Simon restating what she had said on the telephone and also informing him that if he did not comply with these guidelines, she would call the RCMP to have him removed from the school grounds.

26 • Protecting All Students

Janice had had enough of this aggressive parent. She understood where Tyrell's aggression came from. It was time to get tough. Janice informed Tyrell's father that she considered such a threat to be an act of violence by intimidation and that she would not tolerate such behaviour on the school grounds. She warned him against approaching any of her students in a threatening manner. She also told him that if such an incident occurred again, she would contact the police. She also sent a letter to Tyrell's father outlining her concerns and the consequences she had spoken of. She did not hear from Tyrell's father again. The boys kept their distance from each other for the remainder of the school year. Janice was relieved that the incident did not escalate any further. She realized that sometimes the best defence when dealing with a tough individual was to get tough back.

27 • Someone Help Me!

Janice then called the parents of all of the other students who had been involved, explained the situation to them, and asked that they all meet with her at seven o'clock that evening at the school to discuss what had occurred. Amber and her parents elected not to attend. All of the other parents attended the meeting with their son or daughter. They agreed that their children's behaviour was unacceptable no matter what the cause and that this was a parenting and a community issue and not just a school concern. Janice emphasized that they needed to know where their children were after school. Janice followed up the meeting with letters to all of the parents explaining behavioural expectations for the future. The parents thanked Janice for the way she had handled the situation.

28 • Not in This School!

Both administrators agreed to suspend four students involved in the incident for three days. When they returned to school, the students would have to meet with the counsellor and go through a drug and alcohol prevention program with him. The fifth student, who had brought the substance to school, was suspended for the remainder of the school year (about two weeks). She was also obliged to come to the school for the drug and alcohol counselling sessions.

Parents were phoned, amidst many tears, and the suspended students were sent home. The following day, the privilege of leaving the school grounds at lunch hour was revoked for all grade 7 students. Too many of them had been in the park without permission, and, because it was almost the end of the year, the administrators did not want to do any further investigations and to give permission to some students to leave the school and not to others. It would be far too much work for such a short period of time. The students did not like this, but most accepted it without too many complaints.

There were mixed reactions from the parents of the suspended students. One parent said that she agreed with the suspension, but not with the drug and alcohol counselling. Another parent said that her child should have a lesser punishment because she had just held the joint and had not smoked it. The parent of the child who had brought the substance to school was devastated but completely supported the school's decision. One parent was most worried about whether or not this would go on his child's file. He was worried that when his daughter entered her new school the next year, she would already be known as a troublemaker by the staff. The administrators stood by their decision, and the consequences were carried out without further protest.

29 • The Picture

Janice called the superintendent to find out about what she should do next. The superintendent told her that she should not interview any of the children involved. Janice explained that she had already interviewed students to find out if there was any credibility to the story. The superintendent explained that, with any allegations of a sexual nature, the proper course of action would be to let the ministry responsible for children's services handle the investigation. He instructed Janice to contact them immediately and to later inform the superintendent's office of the outcome. She was also to write a letter to the support worker informing him of the allegations and telling him that the matter had been turned over to the appropriate ministry for investigation. The letter was also to inform him that he was suspended from work, pending the outcome of the investigation.

Janice contacted the ministry. They began an investigation and contacted the RCMP. In the end, the ministry informed Janice that while the support worker had exercised poor judgement, there was no evidence to support a charge of child abuse.

30 • What to Do?

Janice learned six months later that Ms. Bright had purchased the morning-after pills and had given them to Yvonne. She chose not to pursue the issue with her.

31 • Shared Decision Making

Janice met with Dave and told him that he had been out of line in calling her staff to speak against the staffing committee and that he was deliberately trying to stir things up. She asked him why he believed it was necessary to make all of these late-night phone calls after the staffing committee was finished. Again, she informed him that Frank, the union president, had supported her staffing committee initiative. He had actually helped Janice work out some of the details. Dave continued to be argumentative, and Janice ended the meeting.

After Frank returned, he phoned Janice and told her that he had met with Dave and had "had it out with him." Frank assured Janice that he would continue to support staffing committees and that he still believed it was an excellent way to involve teachers and parents in the school's decision-making process.

32 • To Skip a Grade?

Janice stayed behind to talk to the teacher. Mrs. Chen felt that she had just been accused of not being a competent educator. Within an hour, Janice received a phone call from the other school requesting Lisa's files. Janice breathed a sigh of relief but couldn't help but think that there would have been a different outcome if the problem with the teacher, student, and parent had been spotted earlier and if clear communication systems had been set up.